Poets on Fortune's Hill

by the same author

*

SHAKESPEARE'S DOCTRINE OF NATURE

POETS ON FORTUNE'S HILL

Studies in
Sidney, Shakespeare,
Beaumont & Fletcher

by

JOHN F. DANBY

KENNIKAT PRESS, INC./PORT WASHINGTON, N. Y.

To
GERTRUDE

POETS ON FORTUNE'S HILL

First Published in 1952
Reissued in 1966 by Kennikat Press

Manufactured in the United States of America
Library of Congress Catalog Card No: 66-25905

Acknowledgements

I wish to thank the Editors of the *Cambridge Journal* for permission to reprint in Chapters 1, 4 and 6 material which first appeared as articles. Similar thanks are due to the Editors of *Scrutiny* for their permission to reprint the study of *Antony and Cleopatra* which constitutes Chapter 5. My other indebtednesses are many. To Dr. E. M. W. Tillyard, for much helpful comment, I owe a great deal, and to Professor Kenneth Muir I am indebted for reading the finished book in MS. Most of my colleagues have been drawn upon, both by way of particular promptings and by way of general stimulus. Particularly I would like to thank Mr. Terence May for drawing my attention to Boethius, and Miss P. Thomson for generously allowing me to see her work (still in progress) on the background of patronage during the period. Mr. W. H. G. Armytage has, again, been a constant source of real help. Finally, I should like to remember Ben and Fay Pomerance and Cedric and Rena Collins for many friendly imponderables, neither literary nor academic in themselves, but without which no books would ever be written.

Contents

POET. *Sir, I have upon a high and pleasant hill*
Feign'd Fortune to be thron'd.
The Base o' th' Mount
Is rank'd with all deserts, all kinde of Natures
That labour on the bosome of this Sphere,
To propagate their states; amongst them all,
Whose eyes are on this Soveraigne Lady fixt,
One do I personate of Lord Timon's *frame,*
Whom Fortune with her Ivory hand wafts to her,
Whose present grace, to present slaves and servants
Translates his Rivals.

PAINTER. *'Tis conceyv'd, to scope.*
This Throne, this Fortune, and this Hill me thinkes
With one man becken'd from the rest below,
Bowing his head against the steepy Mount
To climbe his happinesse, would be well exprest
In our Condition.

POET. *Nay, Sir, but heare me on:*
All those which were his Fellowes but of late,
Some better then his valew; on the moment
Follow his strides, his Lobbies fill with tendance,
Raine Sacrificiall whisperings in his eare,
Make Sacred even his styrop, and through him
Drinke the free Ayre.

PAINTER. *I marry, what of these?*

POET. *When Fortune in her shift and change of mood*
Spurnes down her late beloved; all his Dependants
Which labour'd after him to the Mountaines top,
Even on their knees and hand, let him sit downe,
Not one accompanying his declining foot.

PAINTER. *'Tis common.*
A thousand morall Paintings I can shew
That shall demonstrate these quicke blowes of Fortune,
More pregnantly than words. Yet you do well,
To shew Lord Timon, *that meane eyes have seene*
The foot above the head.

Timon of Athens, Act I, sc. i.

Prologue

When he described Fortune's Hill the Poet in *Timon* was not wittingly speaking as a sociologist of letters. His remarks are, indeed, rather those of a jejune moralist. We intend to wrest the image from its particular application. For us the Hill will provide a kind of model of Elizabethan society. And this is not, I think, doing too great an injustice to the spirit of the Poet's observations. Fortune did single out this man or that for favour. Her favour, however, inevitably expressed itself in terms of social *eminence*. The Poet saw all men's careers as upward and arduous climbs. He knew there was a 'grade' to be 'made'. With *King Lear* in mind, he might also know how lesser men could attach themselves to the 'great wheel' and be hauled up behind it. He knew too the ambiguity in Fortune's favours: that they were neither indifferent nor directly proportionate to 'desert'. The disproportion is the thing: the real and the actual are in a condition of unstable disequilibrium.

There is a further recognition implicit in the scene as Shakespeare handles it. The Poet is soliciting patronage and the rewards a patron can bestow. Shakespeare stands him in the anteroom of the Great House. He is only one of a throng. Around him are merchants, senators, soldiers, gentlemen, 'a Painter, and a Jeweller'.

The Poet did not exhaust the implications of his image. We can legitimately, I think, moralize the Hill in ways he failed to do. The first point would be the importance of patronage in the Elizabethan-Jacobean environment. If one were not oneself either rich or eminent it was imperative to have a backer. This guaranteed one's bread-and-butter, one's status, and one's possible advancement. The patronage might come from a single great Lord, or from one of the Great Houses that sheltered the *élite*, the Elizabethan 'consumers' of culture. (We need to know much more about the distribution of patronage in the families of Sidneys, Herberts, Russells, etc., as well as at the Court.)[1]

In this respect the economy of Letters as a profession in Elizabethan-Jacobean times might still be said to be late-feudal. But this is not the full picture. In another respect we are at the beginning of the modern age. New economic relations are developing within the field of literature. Elizabeth's reign launched the modern entertainment business. The public theatres initiated a minor economic revolution. Drama, in the first instance, was not 'poetry' or even 'literature'. And its patron was a 'public'. So the economy typical of the conditions in which Shakespeare, for example, wrote can best be described as 'mixed'. Shakespeare's own work indicates the mixture: the *Sonnets*, *Venus and Adonis*, and *Lucrece* on the one hand and the plays on the other; Southampton, and the audience of the *Globe*. In this respect as in others Shakespeare belongs to a period transitional between two worlds.

The picture of the Hill of Fortune, and of literature bound to the patronage of either Great House or Public Theatre, already makes the Elizabethan-Jacobean scene less monolithic than it is sometimes imagined. Taking the image further, increasing complications become evident. The Hill has different levels and different sides. Movements up and down, and around and about, or movements combining both these, are possible. Different views are to be expected from different positions on the Hill. Elizabethan society is as highly differentiated as any other. Literature is what happens 'in' a man, certainly. What can happen 'in' him, however, will be partly conditioned by what has happened 'to' him in virtue of his place and behaviour on the Hill. Finally, literature is addressed by a man from his place to those of his contemporaries (on the same Hill) who are in a position to listen to him. Such moralizings are as jejune as those of Timon's Poet. But the commonplaces are important. Literature has a three-dimensional setting. Very often it is reduced in the study to something as two-dimensional as the paper it is written on.

Some of the differences between specific works might best be accounted for in terms of social placing. The *Arcadia* is Great House literature, and Sidney the interpreter of the *ethos* of the Great House. Shakespeare's plays belong to the open town, the open Elizabethan country, and the unroofed commercial theatre. Beaumont and Fletcher are curious hybrids: second-generation scions of the Elizabethan *élite*, and second-generation exploiters of a theatre now no longer, possibly, open to the sky.

Once these differences have been recognized likenesses and differences at deeper levels can sometimes be observed. Thus, to me, Sidney's *Arcadia* has more in common with Shakespeare's *Lear* and *Pericles* than these have with the plays of Beaumont and Fletcher. Shakespeare and Sidney (in ways which remain to be indicated) are somehow members of the same moral community. Beaumont and Fletcher, using the same theatre as Shakespeare, belong to a different world.

It is known that Shakespeare had read Sidney by 1605—at the time when he was writing *King Lear*. It is apparent that shortly after *King Lear* Shakespeare's work undergoes a series of changes more or less abrupt. It has been urged that the new drama of Beaumont and Fletcher must be taken into account in any discussion of the nature of these changes and the reasons for them. One of the motives behind the writing of this book has been the desire tentatively to explore what was happening during Shakespeare's last important transition—the transition from *King Lear* to the final plays. Can it be said to be the 'influence' of Beaumont and Fletcher? Or the impact of Sidney almost a generation after the *Arcadia* was written? And at what level do these 'influences' work? What weight should be attached to the external? And how does the external influence combine with those internal changes that can be assumed to be taking place in an ageing dramatist who seems in *King Lear* to have reached his maximum growth and completest insight? It is from such a centre as this that the studies which follow have emanated.

A recognition of the social placing of the writers concerned helps, I think, towards a clearer view of how matters stand between them on these questions. And not only that. The question of 'influences' ceases to be merely academic, eccentrically driving away from the text. When 'influences' are seen in relation to social placing, and when social place is seen to imply a whole *ethos*, intellectual, temperamental, and spiritual, the question of 'influence' takes on a new significance. It is brought into relation with the essential quality of the work itself, as written by a man from his place. It is, in other words, made relevant to a just appreciation of what the work under consideration *is*, and not merely what it is 'derived' from.

The three-cornered investigation pursued in the studies, as well as the three-dimensionality, imposes a maybe curious pattern of procedure. Sidney's *Arcadia* is the first of the works under consideration to be written. As Great House literature it is also, sociologically, the most archaic. After a general view of the Hill on which the Elizabethan-Jacobean poets worked (Chapter I) it is important to take certain of our bearings from it. Intrinsically, too, the *Arcadia* deserves more serious attention than it has been granted since the end of the seventeenth century. Shakespeare's impact is later than that of Sidney, and his milieu is different. Logically he must be considered next. At this point, however, the chronological procedure is disturbed. *Pericles* is discussed before *King Lear*, and *Antony and Cleopatra* (written after *King Lear* but before *Pericles*) concludes the Shakespearian sequence. *Pericles* is nearest, at one level, to the Sidneian kind of romance, and it is the forerunner of Shakespeare's final period. In the last plays Shakespeare uses 'romance' as in the Roman plays he uses Plutarch. In both the last plays and the Roman plays Shakespeare seems deliberately to adopt self-chosen limits. After *King Lear*, in my view, there is something eclectic in his work. A comparative discontinuity of both tone and content has to be recognized. This is all the more apparent if *King Lear* is turned to immediately after *Pericles*. Both plays handle the great theme of patience, *Pericles* after something of the Sidneian manner (mediated through more popular romances), *King Lear* after Shakespeare's own manner, but within the great positive tradition which comes down to the Elizabethan Everyman from the Middle Ages. Chaucer's Griselde stands behind Shakespeare's Cordelia. Sidney's Philoclea stands by her in the same Elizabethan world: but between Philoclea and Cordelia are the walls of the Great House.

The study of *Antony and Cleopatra* which follows that of Christian Patience in *King Lear* is intended to underline further the break which seems to occur in 1606. From the Christian world of *King Lear* (a world that embraces catastrophe and crucifixion and yet breathes the essence of charity that suffereth long) to the world of North's Plutarch (with its counter-Christian ethic which makes suicide a virtue) is a transition abrupt enough. *Antony and Cleopatra* underlines Shakespeare's eclecticism at this period. It is after Plutarch that Shakespeare turns to the Sidneian, and the Sidneian world is different from either that of Lear or Antony: it is a world where misfortune has its place, but where irremediable catastrophe is impossible, where adversity is a blessing and patience assured of a reward.

Antony and Cleopatra, from another point of view, seems to indicate a new age. But Shakespeare did not characterize this age as clearly as Beaumont. The last studies of the book are of Beaumont's *Philaster* and *The Maid's Tragedy*. With these we enter yet another moral universe, and one which the traditional acceptances, decencies, and heroisms of Sidney and Shakespeare only define by contrast. It is the sphere of the nascent 'cavalier', or, rather, of the rapidly changing society which was to produce first the 'cavalier' and then the Civil War.

CHAPTER ONE

Fortune's Hill and the Poets

Our view of the Elizabethan-Jacobean Hill is confirmed, I think, by Donne in a letter to Sir Henry Goodyer written in 1608—in the period, that is, of *Timon*, *Pericles*, *Antony and Cleopatra*, and Beaumont's *Philaster*. (Donne, of course, has an imagery of his own.)

'I would fain do something, but that I cannot tell what is no wonder. For to choose is to do; but to be no part of any body is nothing. At most the greatest persons are but great wens and excrescences; men of wit and delightful conversation but as moles for ornament, except that they be incorporated into the body of the world that they contribute something to the sustentation of the whole.

'This I made account that I begun early, when I understood the study of our laws; but was diverted by the worst voluptuousness, which is an hydroptic, immoderate desire of human learnings and languages—beautiful ornaments to great fortunes; but mine needed an occupation.'[1]

For us Donne is the master-poet. His contemporaries thought of him as the great Dean of St. Paul's. In this letter we see him as he saw himself: the lawyer without occupation, the scholar without an employer, the courtier without a place, the gentleman without a fortune. His knowledge issues from a complex of frustrations. It is at once a knowledge of himself and an insight into his time. The two things knit together to form a single judgment in a way we associate not with Donne's age (the age of metaphysics and wit) but with our own (the age of mass-observation and statistics). The scene Donne points to had once included Sidney, as its brightest ornament and example. It still included Beaumont and Fletcher. (Donne might stand as a representative of their class. All three are shabby-genteel. Beaumont and Fletcher, however, explore the possibilities of the theatre as patron: Donne is still tied to the single rich man or generous patroness.) Shakespeare too is still part of the scene, but as a successful 'new man' in the new business connected with playwriting. Donne's scene is that of 'the greatest persons' and the 'wits' and the 'body of the world' into which both had to be incorporated. Without incorporation a man will be 'nothing', or else 'lie in a sullen weedy lake'. Inadequacy to a work too large, Donne even feels, would be better than complete inactivity:

'When I must shipwreck, I would do it in a sea where mine impotency might have some excuse; not in a sullen weedy lake, where I would not have so much as exercise for my swimming.'[2]

It is the world of the patrons and their poets and the society which enabled each to get a living. To understand the poet we must understand the setting. Poetry is always written from a place. It becomes what the economists would call 'work' when it gains acceptance and a reward.

The scene Donne looked out on had been shaped in all its most important features by the rapid glacial thaw of the late Middle Ages and the acceleration of this which the sixteenth century witnessed. It was a scene still dominated, even in his time, by four or five renaissance dynasties—Herberts, Cecils, Cavendishes, Russells: almost all of them called into being and maintained in effective place by the creative *fiat* of the Tudor despot. Their stories are allegories of their time.

Of such biographical allegory Aubrey's *Brief Lives*—historical memory working at the brief range of a hundred years or so—is an invaluable repository. Even where his 'gossip' is suspect Aubrey's accounts will sometimes ring true. He has a flair for the spirit of fact rather than the letter. George Herbert and Herbert of Cherbury, for example, were figures of Aubrey's own century. Both went back, as he also knew, to the first earl of Pembroke, William Herbert (1507-70). Black Will Herbert 'could neither write nor read, but had a stamp for his name'. He was, characteristically enough, a 'younger brother':

'a man fighting young fellow. 'Tis certaine he was a servant of the house of Worcester, and wore their blew-coate and badge. My cosen Whitney's great aunt gave him a golden angell when he went to London.'[3]

In London Black Will killed a man and had to flee to France. There his usefulness as a soldier won him the king's favour and Francis I recommended him back to Henry VIII. He made himself equally useful in England at the time of the Dissolution of the Monasteries. Henry gave him the abbey lands of Wilton, made him a Privy Councillor, and he married the sister of Katherine Parr. In the marches he found turbulent and troublesome neighbours, a hostile environment of still feudal marcher lords who obviously regarded the new man as a squatter. Among these was one, Lord Sturton of Sturton, who 'when he went or returned from Sarum (by Wilton was his rode) would sound his trumpetts, and give reproachfull challenging words; 'twas a relique of knighthood errantry.'

Aubrey's account has the force of symbol. His contemporary literary figures are significantly linked to the great dynasts, and these in their turn are followed back to an early sixteenth-century wildness, usefulness, and illiteracy, and then this is thrown against the back-drop of Mallory-esque medievalism. It is a convincing use of the new art of Perspective. And the perspective is true.

Black Will was a soldier. The Cavendishes began as lawyers. The Cecils proved their worth first as lesser court administrators before they became statesmen. The Dudleys were grandees and large-scale venturers but also useful. They supplied what Greville later describes as the strong 'middle wall'[4] between the crown and the turbulent forces the crown had to rule and manage. Donne's 'greatest persons' could fit into the world of the sixteenth century in manifold ways.

The sturdy non-academic type exemplified in the first earl or Pembroke was only one kind of King's man. Equally characteristic were these others we have already mentioned—officers who had the law, the university, or commerce and finance for their background. William Cecil (1520-98), for example, married Mary Cheke, the sister of the famous royal tutor and Greek scholar. His daughter Anne married Edward de Vere, earl of Oxford. Thomas Cecil, his eldest son, became in James's time earl of Exeter. Robert Cecil, the second son, married Elizabeth, daughter of Baron Cobham. William's grandchildren marry into the ancient houses of Clifford and Howard. It is th technique, on a large scale, of the hermit crab.

Queen Elizabeth had the playful habit of nicknaming her courtiers after the beasts in *Aesop's Fables*.[5] The French ambassador was the Ape and Burleigh was her Fox. There is something very fitting in the imagery. Elizabeth's rule was the domination of symbiotic animals held together not by identity of kind, nor by similarity of natures, nor by congeniality of tastes, but by common service—on the same high level—of the queenly lioness.

Symbiosis becomes increasingly characteristic of the sixteenth century. It is maybe best exemplified in the history of the Cavendishes, a house that ultimately furnished Charles I with a general, the great duke of Newcastle—husband to Margaret the cranky Restoration woman of letters, and patron to Jonson, Davenant, Shirley, Dryden, Gassendi, and Hobbes. Sir William Cavendish (1505-57), the founder of the dynasty, was possibly introduced to the court of Henry VIII by his brother George, the friend of Wolsey. He was employed by Henry as commissioner to supervise the surrender of the abbey lands to the crown. He was rewarded with large grants of land from Henry and further grants from Edward. He married (his third wife) a Derbyshire heiress, wisely sold his scattered holdings in order to acquire a large and consolidated estate in Derbyshire, and in 1553 began the building of Chatsworth. He died before Chatsworth was completed, but the work he had begun was finished by his wife at a cost of £80,000. The widow then married the earl of Shrewsbury who had already a family of his own. The young Talbots and Cavendishes were brought up in the same house, and were subsequently, by intermarriage, to forge further links between the old and new: William Cavendish, the son of Sir William, was a justice of peace in 1603, baron in 1605, and earl of Devonshire (for a payment, it was said, of £10,000) in 1618. Thomas Hobbes was employed as tutor to his son.

The hermit crab does not oust or kill off the inhabitant of the shell it will eventually occupy. Along with the new patterns of conduct the old patterns and habits are still to be seen, even as late as 1599. Essex himself might be regarded as the last medievalist. The theology of his outburst to Elizabeth is medieval, and his 'rebellion' the last muster in London of an overlord's private army; Elizabeth striking Essex on the cheek, and Essex's hand flying to his sword, the last flare-up at that level between medieval equals.

On the other hand, while the new nobility could sometimes transform itself completely into the semblance of the old, there were compensatory adoptions by the old nobility of the worst sycophancies of the new. The letters of Henry Howard, for example, counterbalance the rashness and independence of Essex's temper. The ultimate organization of the Howard clan in the court of the Scottish king on the English throne shows how far such transformation could go. But even such behaviour as Henry Howard's was a result of the Tudor design: Henry Howard's father had been beheaded by Elizabeth.

The decay of the feudal class and the rise of the new gentry were thus, on the whole, compensatory movements. The old was made opportunist and trained in the qualities necessary for survival by the new; the new was endowed with the permanence and prestige of the old. The typical renaissance attitude to cosmic change and interchange is always ambivalent:

> . . . *I have seen the hungry ocean gain,*
> *Advantage on the kingdom of the shore,*
> *And the firm soil win of the watery main,*
> *Increasing store with loss and loss with store.*[6]

What has to be remembered, I think, more often than it sometimes is when such questions are discussed, is that the class of the 'greatest men'—that class which was likely to dispense patronage, and certainly held the keys to preferment, the class too for which literature is presumed to have been sometimes written—this class was extremely mixed. It had all the surprising variety of a menagerie rather than the amazing sameness of a herd. It is doubtful, in fact, if the concept of 'class'—a concept both in logic and in sociology which is mainly applicable to herds—can be applied in this instance. It is maybe better to use the Aesopian imagery. The owl and the rat and the snake inhabit the same den. The group raised up around the Tudor throne is heterogeneous. Anyone placed in the group would be likely to have a highly individual and distinctive view. Situation—his particular placing—would account for much.

Heterogeneous as the group was, it did apparently think of itself as being definitely a group. The principle of unity was provided by the figure which dominated all the perspectives of the court servants—that of the Prince. Society, in moving on from the Middle Ages, had replaced *status* as its organizing principle and substituted *usefulness*. The national state was also a rational state. In Fulke Greville's phrase it was the rule of choice not chance. The sixteenth century heralds the appearance of the managerial element in political affairs. The demands of the expanding mercantile-and-national unit were varied and complicated. They required a central controller and this demand was satisfied by the Prince. Arguments as to whether the Privy Council ruled through the Queen, or the Queen through the Privy Council, are largely academic; they are certainly not true to the psychology of Elizabeth's last ten years. The Prince was, or had to be thought to be, the arbiter of usefulness and the rewarder of faithful service. The grandees were touchy of admitting that they received gifts from anyone who was a subject. The throne was the seat of absolute power, of final veto, of the snap judgment and revolutionary decision which the new society in the process of formation needed so urgently. The Prince was the centre of the state organization, its consciousness of acting by choice rather than chance.

It is for this reason that the renaissance despot is so often talked of in terms nearly approaching blasphemy. It is not always that the distinction between God and king can be so clearly retained as it is by Greville:

'God creates those in his certain, and eternall mouldes, out of which he elects for himself; where Kings choose creatures out of *Pandora's* tun, and so raise up worth and no worth.'[7]

At the time when he writes this of course Greville is not as yet James's Privy Councillor: he is the frustrated Elizabethan diplomatist and man of action, the arm-chair playwright and moralistic puritan poet, the would-be historian of his time denied access to the original sources by Salisbury's jealousy for the state top-secrets. Daniel, on the other hand, the future Gentleman of the Bedchamber, endows kingship with the very highest attributes:

God gives to Kings the honour to command,
To subjects, all their glory to obay;
Who ought in time of war as rampiers stand,
In peace as th' ornaments of State aray.
The King hath recompens'd your services
With better love than you show thankfulnesse.
By grace he made you greater than you were
By nature, you receiv'd that which he was not tide
To give you: his gift was far more deere
Than all you did: in making you imployd.[8]

The king is not only the disburser of abbey lands and titles, he is in a very real sense the new treasury of merit. Elizabeth herself rarely forgot the theological and social importance of Works: she insisted on returns of usefulness for her favours. By James's time (maybe reflecting, by compensation, the diminishing role of the king as compared with that of his Privy Council) the king's grace is recklessly and arbitrarily bestowed. The treasurer of merit is the centre of a state lottery for favour.

The Prince, then, dominated the whole scene in the mind of the ruling class in the sixteenth and early seventeenth centuries. He dominated too that literature which was written from this class, or with an eye on its patronage. Before proceeding to examine the placing of the various groups of sixteenth- and seventeenth-century writers, we might conclude this preliminary short view of the body of their time by recalling Fulke Greville's judicial assessment.

Greville's *Life of Sidney* is an important document. It is consciously written from a point of view. It is courtier's history done by an Elizabethan who has not yet found his place under James. It is informed by a sense of pattern, the sense of choice not chance. It is deliberately composed and by intention exists to render homage to a time of greatness that is gone. All the same it is a shrewd analytic statement of the mechanics of sixteenth-century rule written from the inside by a man who knows the works. It presents two heroic types, Sir Philip Sidney and Queen Elizabeth, the ideal man of letters and the ideal Prince. In each case Greville seems to be interpreting the intentions of his time.

For the first time in English history all the parts of the body politic are conceived as instruments. Society is a machine that requires manipulation and control. For Greville, Elizabeth is the master-mistress of the new art of manipulation which good government has become. Not power but the ability to use and manipulate powers is the secret of her success: she is in government what Sidney is in literature:

'a quintessence of abilities, gathered out of those blessed and blessing mixtures of Nature, Education, and Practice, which never faile to lift up man above man, and keep him there, more than place or power shall by any other encroaching advantages ever be able to do.'[9]

Greville sees clearly that James's 'encroaching advantages' are no substitute for Elizabeth's innate genius. The danger in the new society, for the Prince, is that he is always able to forge an instrument for himself but might not always be able to control it. Elizabeth avoided the danger, where James, Greville hints, did not. The nemesis of failure for the Prince is that in such a case he might become the tool of his own creations. Elizabeth operated, however, by working on the jealousies of the competing appetites: as Ulysses did on Ajax and Achilles. Thus the head of the armed forces was offset by someone put at his side to act as a constant check:

'to allay that vast power of place with some insensible counterpoise, (she) many times joyned an active Favorite with that Sea-

Neptune of hers, making credit, place, and merit, finely competitors in her service.'[10]

Yet Elizabeth never permitted herself a 'Monopolous use of Favourites', nor (which would amount to the same thing) her favourites a monopolous use of her, 'as if she would make any greater than herself, to governe Tyrannically by them'.[11]

Throughout Greville's account we are constantly reminded of the Greek camp in *Troilus and Cressida*. 'Credit, place, and merit' are significant conjunctions. Nor is Greville being cynical. Like Ulysses he is merely being perceptive: neither credit, place, nor merit need have any connexions with each other. Separately they are the competing factors of high birth, honest desert, and reputation. More often than not (as Shakespeare noted in his sonnet) they are mutually exclusive. Only in Elizabeth do all three actually cohere. Wherever any one of them is found, however, and there is a use for it, the Prince will use it. Nor can that usefulness be expected to establish a claim on the Prince. He will not be grateful. Rather, like Ulysses' Time, the Prince

. . . hath, my lord, a wallet at his back
Wherein he puts alms for oblivion,
A great-sized monster of ingratitudes:
Those scraps are good deeds past, which are devour'd
As fast as they are made, forgot as soon
As done: perseverance, dear my lord,
Keeps honour bright: to have done is to hang
Quite out of fashion, like a rusty mail
In monumental mockery. Take the instant way:
For honour travels in a straight so narrow
Where one but goes abreast: keep then the path;
For emulation hath a thousand sons
That one by one pursue: if you give way,
Or hedge aside from the direct forthright,
Like to an enter'd tide they all rush by
And leave you hindmost. . . .
. . . O let not virtue seek
Remuneration for the thing it was;

For beauty, wit,
High birth, vigour of bone, desert in service,
Love, friendship, charity, are subjects all
To envious and calumniating time.[12]

At a period when international policy was adopting a similar world-view, Greville saw both the microcosm of man and the macrocosm of society as a counterbalancing of powers presided over and ordered by reason. Elizabeth's art was a baroque achievement: a reconciliation of geometry and bursting opportunist vitality. Government was the rational use of an assortment of irrationals—the brute data of blood, inherited place, natural endowment, practical experience, the younger son and the elder son, bastard or un-bastard. There is a significant equalization of hitherto disparate things in Greville's analysis. All are equal under the Prince: all wait for their adoption, for the opportunity to be given, for the usefulness they will be allowed to express. The Elizabethan world-picture for him is not an undynamic stratification of 'degree'. Rather it resembles the mad race Ulysses also describes. The competitors are ignorant while they are running of the handicapper's initial decisions. They only know that over-success might be penalized as much as indifferent performance. The master-mistress is interested not so much in winners as in having a good field and in readiness and ability to run.

In his account of the Tudor scene Greville avoids the two main dangers. He does not make the Prince the absolute and single maintainer of the régime. She is not in herself 'power' but the manipulator of powers. Nor does he, with the economic determinists, reduce the role of the individual Prince to that of mere figurehead. (Men can be both more determined and more vacillating than economic laws.) Greville is aware on the one hand of the independent forces that had to be controlled, and on the other of the part played by the executive Prince in controlling and manipulating them. We might stick to the image of the race. Society is a competition of strong runners, some of them born to be favourites and for a time to lead the field. The Prince, however, is handicapper, judge, and purse-holder. What Greville calls Elizabeth's technique of 'insensible counterpoise' her servants would only recognize as rule by prizes.

Such then, conceivably, was the 'body of the world' into which the poets had to be incorporated. It was a world dominated by the 'greatest persons' as these were also dominated by the centralizing throne. Among the 'greatest persons' would be people like Timon, and others like Ulysses and Nestor, attempting to yoke together the Elephant and the Bull and make beef-wit implement a rational policy. It was a world of strong runners and big prizes. The poets sometimes—though rarely—were themselves of the class of the 'greatest persons'. More often they were seeking attachment to the great wheel going up the hill. They depended on patronage, if not (as in Donne's case in 1608) for the very means of livelihood, certainly for advancement. Let us glance now at the social placing of representative poets: the placing itself might explain something in the content, tone, and form of the literary output of the time.

The first type is that of the poet above the need for patronage, and with no desire to cater for any audience but himself. Supremely careful of his poetry, he cares nothing for print or for common acclamation. Anxious to achieve greatness, he is anxious about nothing else. The conditions for such a purity of poetic motive are so strict that they exclude all but the most favoured in Nature, Education, and Practice, in credit, place, and merit. Fulke Greville could only think of one such—the equivalent in poetry of Elizabeth in politics: Sir Philip Sidney.

Sidney is unique, but he is also typical. He realizes what was taken to be the ideal for poetry throughout the polite world of the renaissance. This involved the possession of qualifications quite unpoetic in essence. The first was riches. And Sidney was rich enough and eminent enough to be above patronage. He was himself in fact a patron. His poetry thus becomes an aspect of his own magnanimity, a self-dedication, a free gift.

Sidney was also fully incorporated into the body of his world. As soldier, statesman, scholar, and diplomatist, he was a useful man. He combined, like Elizabeth, 'quintessential qualities'. He was great not only in place, but in nature and intellect. In Greville's portrait he is the all-round great man of the renaissance ideal. Poetry for him is certainly not a livelihood and not quite a vocation. It is the expression of many-sidedness, the element finally completing the fullness of the great man.

The content of Sidney's literary work seems to fit the position the poet occupied. The *Apologie* promulgates the notion of 'erected wit'; poetry is the loftiest form of human activity. Poems—such as *Astrophel and Stella*—are definitions of virtue freely espoused. Or else Sidney writes such an heroíc pastoral as the *Arcadia*, regarded by Greville as a kind of text-book for kings and great men:

'in all these creatures of his making, his intent, and scope was, to turn the barren Philosophy precepts into pregnant Images of life; and in them, first on the Monarch's part, lively to present the growth, state, and declination of Princes, change of government, and lawes: vicissitudes of sedition, faction, succession, confederacies, plantations, with all the errors, or alterations in publique affaires. Then again in the subjects case; the state of favor, disfavor, prosperitie, adversity, emulation, quarrel, undertaking, retiring, hospitality, travail, and all other moodes of private fortunes or misfortunes.'[13]

The man placed as Sidney was is in a sense free. Such an aristocrat, as Chesterton would say, is the true democrat. Poetry begins for him at the point where the use-able and the bread-and-butter-minded end. In such poetry the state has withered away. The result is the disinterestedness, directness, and sincerity—the essential truthfulness—which Dr. Bronowski[14] points to. Poetry is self-discipline and self-realization: the fashioning of a 'second nature'. As Greville says:

'But the truth is, his end was not writing, even while he wrote; nor his knowledge moulded for tables, or schooles; but both his wit, and understanding bent upon his heart, to make himself and others, not in words or opinion, but in life and action, good and great. In which Architectonicall art he was . . . a Master.'[15]

For Fulke Greville Sidney was 'that exact image of quiet and action'—the happy union of life and letters in renaissance *virtue*. His poetry was equally above the need for patronage or the necessity to publish. His learning was not 'moulded for tables, or schooles'. The professionalism that will use knowledge and skill as a means to a career or to enhanced social prestige are equally distant from it. Poetry and learning are for the purposes of realizing a life rather than obtaining a living. Greville is speaking for more than himself when he confesses that, in his own endeavours, he took Sidney for a model and set himself 'to saile by his compasse', particularly to achieve, if possible, *Ironia*—the literary virtue of holding yourself above professionalism:

'that hypocriticall figure *Ironia*, wherein men commonly (to keep their workes) seeme to make toies of the utmost they can doe.'[16]

Like Timon in the Poet's fable, Sidney had been beckoned by Fortune to the top of her hill. Sidney's example influenced many others. They, however—as Greville admitted in his own case—did not occupy the pinnacle which conferred complete freedom and singleness of mind. They were on various levels lower down the social slope, 'bowing their heads against the steepy mount to climb their happiness'. The next class of poet, then, after Sidney, is the class of those for whom poetry is not truth, or truth alone, but truth with an admixture of something else—something which, speaking generally, might be called prestige: it has to do, anyway, with the atmosphere of the great persons, with the competition for favour and patronage, with that which led Donne to see the 'men of wit but as moles for ornament'.

The greatest member of this class is, of course, Edmund Spenser. Here again Aubrey's story, even if it is not factually probable, has a kind of symbolic appositeness. He tells how Spenser took his poetry along to Sidney to be read. Spenser was kept waiting in the ante-room so long he thought the great man had forgotten his existence. Actually, Aubrey goes on to say, Sidney was at that very moment engrossed by the Spenser he was reading. The difference in social status between the two, however, could not be more strongly stated.[17]

It is likely that Spenser—a scholar, not too rich, but well

connected—was given an introduction to Sidney on the strength of his poetry. It is more likely, I think, that his introduction was the outcome of his general culture and possible usefulness. One of the needs generated by the sixteenth-century nation-state was the need for servants with a classical education, knowledge of the main western European languages, and a taste for history and the practical conduct of affairs. Fulke Greville was such a man, and so was Sir Henry Wootton. Spenser would find ready incorporation into the body of the Sidney-Leicester-Raleigh world on the strength of similar qualifications. He was sixteenth-century 'foreign office' type. His literary capacity would be an extra qualification. It is known, at any rate, that he lived in close association with both Sidney and Leicester and that he gained a post as secretary to Lord Grey of Wilton, went to Ireland, was granted land, returned in the early nineties with the first three books of the *Faerie Queene*, went back to Ireland again, wrote three more books of his national epic, was burned out in the troubles of 1598, and died in England in reduced circumstances. His position as Grey's secretary might be regarded as the direct outcome of the Sidney-Leicester patronage. The *Faerie Queene* might be regarded as a bid for the direct patronage of Elizabeth herself, to whom it is dedicated: 'the most high, mightie, and magnificent Empresse, renowned for pietie, vertue, and all gratious government.' Elizabeth, of course, took homage for granted, and was cautious in her disbursements of largesse. In 1598, however, Spenser secured appointment as Sheriff of Cork.

The symbiosis of sixteenth-century society is reflected on the literary level. Spenser's verse is a particularly good example of the amalgam that results. In the *Faerie Queene* the matter of King Arthur consorts with the allegory of Mary Queen of Scots, the ethics of Aristotle with the machinery of the Seven Deadly Sins, medieval morality with renaissance epic theory, naïve Chaucerisms with abstruse platonizings, the portraying of an ideal virtue with the flattery of an ageing queen. On a small scale we can see the amalgam almost anywhere in *The Shepherds Calendar*:

Of fayre Elisa be your silver song,
That blessed wight,
That flower of Virgins: may she flourish long
In princely plight!
For she is Syrinx daughter without spotte,
Which Pan, the Shepherds God, of her begot:
So sprong her grace
Of heavenly race,
No mortal blemishe may her blotte.

See, where she sits upon the grassie greene,
(O seemely sight!)
Yclad in Scarlot, like a Mayden Queene,
And ermines white:
Upon her head a Cremosin coronet,
With Damaske roses and Daffadillies set:
Primroses betweene,
And bay leaves greene,
Embellish the sweete Violet.[18]

Spenser's is the poetry of accretion and accumulation, the poetry of display. It exists to be conspicuous and rich at once. It addresses itself to a coterie such as could derive—among many things else—the coterie pleasure of 'recognition': recognition of the sources ransacked to provide ingredients for the amalgam. It is poetry deliberately and professionally compounded.

Spenser is different in this from Sidney, and the difference has to do, I think, in part, in addition to the difference in their endowments, with the difference in their poetic situation as members of their community. Sidney is on the top of Fortune's hill, whereas Spenser is not. Spenser's poetry must win him preferment, and then maintain him in place in the body of the world. For Sidney poetry is the private devotion to truth. For Spenser it must also be the public vindication of his claim to recognition as a poet, a proof that the poet as such is engaged on work of national importance.

There is therefore in Spenser a professional earnestness, an earnestness not only about 'truth' but also an earnestness to display his command over all the poetic crafts. His poetry requires the external occasion, the prescriptions of theory and form, the suggested topic; and in its most ambitious assay of skill it will load story with allegory, and allegory with morality, and morality with platonism, to form a massive assembly of all the by-products of renaissance learning and art. Spenser is in no position to display the literary virtue Greville called *Ironia*. He will not rise above the apparatus of learning itself and poetic craft in itself and submit both to the need to express the truth or nothing. He will not 'make a toie of the utmost he can doe'. His tactics will in fact be the opposite of this. His art will be a highly professional exhibition. Spenser is 'the poet's poet'. Where Sidney was writing for himself Spenser was writing for an audience: an audience, however, sage, sophisticated, serious, and civilized. He is the poet poeticizing in public.

For Sidney, we have said, poetry was truth, whereas for Spenser poetry was prestige. The prestige involved was multiple. First there was the poet's own; second, that of his patrons; third, that of his country. At Spenser's level English literature becomes involved in the international rivalry of the sixteenth-century *Kulturkampf*. It is the scope of Spenser's undertaking in writing the *Faerie Queene*, and his success in demonstrating that the resources of English culture were capable of producing something as impressive as Ariosto or Tasso, which makes for this greatness. The Spenserians after Spenser, still writing largely within the shade of Sidneian patronage, can pastoralize and poeticize, but cannot lift the enormous poetic weights with which Spenser juggled; nor are they so various or so learned, or so deft or mellifluous in their transitions. It is by comparing Spenser with the Spenserians that we can appreciate his greatness most easily.

Sidney was himself a great man and a patron. Spenser—like lesser poets that seem to fit into the same situational group: Daniel, Drayton, William Browne—secured incorporation into the world where he had to win bread by attaching himself to the great house. Donne represents a third type. He is the gentleman-poet who is also, in the non-pejorative sense, and as he himself feels acutely in his letter, a misfit:

But I remaine a poyson'd fountaine still.[19]

His life seems a succession of bold bids for high prizes which never came off. The Islands Voyage in which he was involved with Essex disappointed everybody. His marriage, the hardiest of his gambles, made his prospects worse afterwards than before. His application for the secretaryship of the Virginia Company was fruitless. At last, after he had thus failed to find an opening in the Army, the Court, the Government, or Commerce, a place was found for him in the Church.

Donne's poetry yokes together contrary ideas by violence. Two of those ideas—and those over which most violence is displayed in the yoking—are the idea of the poet as 'nothing', 'no part of any body', and the idea of the great persons who, in Donne's world, seem to be everything:

For, Reason, *put t'her best* Extension,
Almost meetes Faith, *and makes both* Centres *one:*
And nothing ever came so neer to This,
As Contemplation *of the PRINCE we misse.*[20]

Throughout the bulk of Donne's adulatory verse we see him desperately lashing and knotting these two together—the hydroptically learned poet who is poor and the fantastically rich patroness who is kind. Donne did not rate his poetry high among the reasons why he should be favoured. The knowledge which the Countess of Bedford had of him, he writes, 'was in the beginning of a graver course, than of a Poet, into which (that I may also keep my dignity) I would not seem to relapse'.[21] His poetry, however, he seems consistently to have used as a means of leverage. It helped to secure entry into the great house. Or, it grappled the rich prize to his heart with hoops of conceits.

Donne was not merely the victim of bad luck. He carried several handicaps which would make it difficult for him to secure adoption. First, there was his catholicism: though this was not, in the nineties, an automatic disqualification, it was not in any way a positive advantage. Then, Donne was not a Sidneian by gifts, place, or inclination. Again, in addition to being outside the orbit of Penshurst and Wilton, he was too genteel (unlike Drayton) for occasional hack-work in the public theatres. He was born, too, fifteen years too early to take advantage, as the similarly genteel Beaumont and Fletcher did, of the changed theatrical and social conditions of 1606-10. He cultivated instead, throughout the last years of Elizabeth's reign, the dark side of late-Elizabethan poetry—the anti-idealist song and sonnet, the anti-social and rather frowned-upon satire: a *genre* Spenser turned to only once in his corrosive *Mother Hubberd's Tale*, and Drayton (when he too was disappointed) in the *Owl*. The significant thing about Donne would seem to be that in him the usual order was reversed. He comes to the adulatory letters and obsequies after he has felt the full bitterness of defeat.

Ben Jonson found something rather shocking in Donne's *Anniversaries*: they were 'prophane and full of blasphemies'.[22] A commentator in 1909 had the same reaction, only mildly qualified:

'Transfigured as they are by imaginative power, they yet betray unmistakeable signs of the effort to bid high. The verses reached their mark, and Donne became for many years the intimate friend and dependant of the wealthy Sir Robert Drury.'[23]

It is easy to explain the shockingness away. Donne's own answer to Jonson, for example, was that 'he described the Idea of a Woman, and not as she was'. To Magdalen Herbert he wrote:

'and of the grossest flattery there is this good use, that they tell us what we should be.'[24]

Or, again:

'There is some of the honour and some of the degrees of a Creation to make a friendship of nothing.'[25]

It is the last phrase which gives the clue to the situation in the epistles and obsequies. It not only repeats the 'nothing' which Donne supposed himself to be for the purpose of writing such addresses. It represents, too, the patroness under the figure of the Creator—that figure which, before, had been used in the Sonnet sequences for the ideal woman as such (the Astrea or Delia or Diana), or, in state eulogy, for Elizabeth herself, or—among Donne's contemporaries at this time—for James, the new treasury of merit and fountain of grace. Sidney's sonnets to Penelope Rich, however, or Drayton's verse to Anne Goodere, are written in a special convention, and are different in tone and intention from Donne's. At their best they make a sincere analysis of Love and 'base affection', they present for inspection the developing drama of sustained personal relation. Within the frame of the convention adopted they retain, or achieve, honesty. In the same way Spenser's poem on Eliza avoids any suggestion of offensiveness or sycophancy. The pastoral setting provided a scale to fit into which the great person had first of all to be *reduced*. After that reduction, and within the setting, adulation achieved the innocence of an at least expected politeness, sometimes a kind of fresh daintiness, sometimes a kind of dignity. In the passage already quoted, for example, the Queen is a nice composition of country girl, 'flower of Virgins', and heaven-born nymph; a pastoral Flora, a stately court Lady, a queen of the May:

Upon her head a Cremosin coronet,
With Damaske roses and Daffadillies set:
Primroses betweene
And bay leaves greene
Embellish the sweete Violet.

Donne's *Verse Letters* are not based on an initial reduction. Nor is the patroness addressed in the letter merely included in the design of a poem composed for a purpose other than flattery. Donne's assumption is the relationship of poet to patron as of nothing to Everything, and out of this he spins his conceits direct. He makes metaphysics out of the poet and patron relation, and a poet-patron relation out of metaphysics:

So you, as woman, one doth comprehend,
And in the vaile of kindred others see;
To some ye are reveal'd, as in a friend,
And as a vertuous Prince farre off, to mee.

To whom, because from you all vertues flow,
And 'tis not none, to dare contemplate you,
I, which does so, as your true subject owe
Some tribute for that, so these lines are due.

If you can think these flatteries, they are,
For then your judgement is below my praise,
If they were so, oft, flatteries work as farre,
As Counsells, and as farre th'endeavour raise.

So my ill reaching you might then grow good,
But I remaine a poyson'd fountaine still,
And not your beauty, vertue, knowledge, blood
Are more above all flattery, than my will.

And if I flatter any, 'tis not you
But my owne judgement, who did long agoe
Pronounce, that all these beauties should be true,
And vertue should your beauty, 'and birth outgrow'.[26]

Behind the relation of poet to patron is set the relation of subject to Prince, behind that the relation of abject and particular many to sublime and universal One, and behind that again the relation of sinner to God. By what Ben Jonson felt to be a peculiar perversity the larger issues are called in to subserve the lesser. It is not reduction but inflation which is Donne's aim: and 'if it were the Virgin Mary, it were somewhat'.

Donne's letters seem to repeat the rituals of conspicuous waste and extravagant display on the poetic level. His account of what he is doing and why is similar to Kenelm Digby's in his *Memoirs* —that transmogrification of the raw material of autobiography into platonic romance of a generation later. Venetia Stanley was in a different category from Lucy Russell (the Venetian Ambassador had called her quite plainly a whore). Digby, however, is resolved that she too shall be the Ideal Woman. He expounds the theory that Love is a gift of the will, and an analogue of the inward relations existing between the Persons of the Godhead. In effect it is a creative *fiat* falling within the subject's prerogative:

'for the ground of it is in ourselves, and we need the help of no exterior thing to make it complete, it dependeth on our wills which we govern as we please: therefore, this is the true happiness that a wise man ought to aim at, since that himself is master of it and he can give it to himself when he list.'[27]

Donne's 'own judgement' operated in the same way when it

did long agoe
Pronounce, that all these praises should be true.

Digby makes one further interesting statement concerning the mechanics and motivation of this second-generation idealism: it is the very best training ground for cavalier loyalty to the King:

'His master, the Prince himself, cannot choose but think well of a servant who shows so good an effect of his loyalty and good nature that nothing (i.e. even unfaithfulness on her part) can make him false to her he loveth.'[28]

Or, as Donne hints:

To some ye are reveal'd, as in a friend,
And as a vertuous Prince farre off to mee.

The bulk of Donne's adulatory verse belongs to the reign of James. And it was during this period (particularly, if one might be definite, during the partnership of Beaumont and Fletcher on the stage) that the cavalier mentality was shaped in all its essentials. Donne's adulatory verse belongs to this formative period. *Mutatis mutandis* Donne's performance in his verse letters is on all fours with that of Beaumont and Fletcher in their plays. Where Jonson could not stomach the blasphemies and profanities of the one, Coleridge was equally revolted by the trickery of the others—whom he liked to characterize best as 'the theorists of Divine Right'. Behind Donne's *Letters* is the desperate plight of the unemployed, of the man who 'would fain do something, but . . . I cannot tell what', of the man who knows that 'to be no part of any body is nothing'. Around this 'nothing' are the 'greatest persons' who are Everything. Over them is the King who in a real sense 'has some of the degrees of a Creation to make a friendship of nothing'. Above the King is stretched the canopy of Divine Right. In such a situation a cynical view of the poetry of the future Dean of St. Paul's would be in the worst possible taste. At the same time, what is true of Beaumont and Fletcher is also true of Donne. In them it is apparent that emotion is in excess of situation. Their stunting with 'impossible' ethical twists is admitted. The same is largely true of Donne. In both it is the initial assumptions behind the brilliant constructs we object to.

The tone of Donne's Epistles is in strong contrast with that of Ben Jonson's:

If, Sackvile, all that have the power to do
Great and good turns, as well could time them too,
And knew their how and where; we should have then
Less list of proud, or ingrateful men.
For benefits are owed with the same mind
As they are done, and such returns they find:
You then, whose will not only, but desire
To succour my necessities, took fire,
Not at my prayers, but your sense; which laid
The way to meet what others would upbraid,
And in the act did so my blush prevent,
As I did feel it done as soon as meant;
You cannot doubt but I who freely know
This good from you, as freely will it owe;
And though my fortune humble me to take
The smallest courtesies with thanks, I make
Yet choice from whom I take them; and would shame
To have such do me good I durst not name.
They are the noblest benefits, and sink
Deepest in man, of which when he doth think,
The memory delights him more, from whom
Than what, he hath received. Gifts stink from some.[29]

This is nobler poetry than Donne's. From the same subject Jonson educes different implications. The relation of grateful poet to magnanimous patron is taken for granted and full justice done to its normal and necessary requirements. At the same time the relation itself—the particular and accidental thing—is given a further relation to the universal structure of the permanent dignities of man. The transaction is two-sided, but on both sides it is the same image of man that must express itself in the giving and receiving. It is this image which is greater than the poet, and greater than the patron too. Without displaying the agility of an overt design on metaphysical conceit, Jonson can bind particular and universal together and throng his lines with the subtle overtones of humane sense:

> *You cannot doubt but I who freely know*
> *This good from you as freely will it owe.*

The poet and the patron—in all but the inessentials—confront each other as equals.

Jonson asserted the dignity of letters in actions as well as words. Samuel Johnson's letter to Lord Chesterfield merely completes the work begun by Ben Jonson at Salisbury's dinner-table in 1606 or 1607:

'Being at the end of my Lord Salisburie's table with Inigo Jones, and demanded by my Lord, Why he was not glad? My Lord, said he, yow promised I should dine with yow, bot I doe not, for he had none of his meate; he esteemed onlie that his meate which was of his own dish.'[30]

This is another incident which, as reported, has the force of symbol. It points to the emergence of the poet-oligarch—the counterpart in the literary sphere to the Cecils in the governmental. For as the Cecils and Cavendishes are the seventeenth-century precursors of the Whig rulers in the eighteenth century, Jonson is already at the same time preparing the position from which the subsequent dictatorships of Dryden and Pope will be exercised. Sidney had assumed that the great man should also be the great poet. Ben Jonson makes the logical deduction that the great man who is not a great poet is only equivalent, and certainly not superior, to the great poet who is not a great man.

Unlike Donne's, Ben Jonson's career is a success story. The young bricklayer is heard discoursing learnedly by one of the Masters of the Inner Temple, sent away to be educated, returns to write *Everyman In*, etc., wins immediate success, is taken up by the new court of James into the more lucrative position of writer of Masques, becomes poet-laureate, associates freely with the great, and when he dies has tribute paid by one of the greatest—Lucius Carey, Viscount Falkland:

To him how daily flockt, what reverence gave
All that had wit, or would be thought to have . . .
How the wise, too, did with mere wits agree,
As Pembroke, Portland, and grave Aubigny.[31]

Ben Jonson is the fourth type of Elizabethan-Jacobean poet. What marks him off from Sidney is that he is a bricklayer who must work with his pen. What marks him off from Spenser is that he descends upon Court and Great House as an outsider who feels himself the equal of any he might find inside:

Nor, when I take my lodging, need I pray
For fire, or lights, or livery; all is there;
As if thou then wert mine, or I reigned here.[32]

What marks him off from Donne is a sense, in itself metaphysical, for the transcendent and yet normal order of decencies to which the poet-patron relation must be subordinated, and which both poetry and society must interpret. Jonson turns his back on the pastoral convention and on the conceit. In his verse addresses he takes up instead the grand human imagery of actual persons in their living relation with him and with the image of man. In doing so he opens out the field which Dryden and Pope will explore further. We are apt to forget nowadays the extent to which it is not Spenser or Donne, but Ben Jonson who dominated the literary past of the eighteenth century.

What gave Ben Jonson his sense of security and independence, of course, was, more than anything else, the fact that when he invaded the field of the 'greatest persons' he had already conquered a territory which would assure him of a livelihood, and over which the greatest persons had little direct hold. All during the age of the Pembrokes and Bedfords and Cavendishes the patron had a powerful rival in the already commercially organized world of the public theatres. There is therefore a fifth type of poet to be reckoned with n the literary scene from 1580–1610: the type which makes its livelihood in the theatre, the theatre as a good business investment, offering a steady job to anyone who could secure enrolment in the protected companies of players, holding out too the constant chance of extras in the way of windfalls from patronage, and—if you could turn out two plays a year—the equivalent in additional income of a skilled craftsman's wages. The best example of this class of writer is, of course, Shakespeare. But Shakespeare's twofold quality (as representative of the country-town and of Elizabethan London, and as unself-conscious heir to a natural morality that has come down from Chaucer) will best be appreciated when we have examined the *Arcadia* and had an opportunity to put beside the conscious Sidneian synthesis the Shakespearian resolutions of *King Lear*. Beaumont and Fletcher (like Donne in some respects, but espousing as a way of preferment the theatre rather than the Church) can await our attention later.

CHAPTER TWO

Sidney's *Arcadia:* the Great House Romance

Professor G. M. Trevelyan cites the advice of 'an old gentleman' (born in 1580) to his grandson. The old man ends what he has to say about books as follows: 'When I was young it was a defect not to be versed in Sir Philip Sidney. . . . To refresh yourself with poetical stories you may take Sir Philip Sidney instead of all.'[1] Sidney's reputation continued high. Charles I had the *Arcadia* by him during his imprisonment. He was said to have read the prayer of one of the Arcadian heroines the night before his death. In *Eikonoklastes* Milton seizes on the alleged fact, and his scorn spills over from the King on to 'the vain amatorious poem' Charles had occupied himself with during his last devotions:

'a book in that kind full of worth and wit, but among religious thoughts and duties not worthy to be named; nor to be read at any time without good caution, much less in time of trouble and affliction to be a Christian's prayer-book.'[2]

Actually, Milton here is being carried away too far. Charles' instinct accorded both with seventeenth-century tradition and with the author's original intention. Sidney's purpose, as Fulke Greville saw it in 1611, had been:

'to limn out such exact pictures, of every posture in the minde, that any man being forced, in the straines of his life, to pass through any straights, or latitudes of good, or ill fortune, might (as in a glasse) see how to set a good countenance upon all the discountenances of adversitie, and a stay upon the exorbitant smilings of chance.'[3]

In this Greville agrees with the general tenour of Sidney's own comment on such a poem—or such a 'heroical romance'—as the *Odyssey:*

'For indeede Poetrie ever setteth vertue so out in her best cullours making Fortune her wel-wayting handmayd, that one must need be enamored of her. Well may you see *Ulisses* in a storme, and in other hard plights; but they are but exercises of patience and magnanimitie, to make them shine the more in the neere-following prosperitie.'[4]

'Patience and magnanimitie', the conjunction of the Christian and the Nicomachean ethic—the phrase indicates something of the seriousness with which Sidney habitually addressed himself to letters, and something of the scope and content of the 'absolute heroicall Poem' he would himself eventually compose. The passage Charles was reading, for example, is introduced as follows:

'Pamela did walk up and down, full of deep, though patient thoughts. For her look and countenance was settled, her pace soft, and almost still of one measure, without any passionate gesture, or violent motion: till at length, as it were awaking, and strengthening herself; "Well," said she, "yet this is the best, and of this I am sure, that howsoever they wrong me, they cannot over-master God: no darkness blinds his eyes, no jail bars Him out. To whom then else should I fly, but to Him for succour?" and therewith kneeling down even where she stood, she thus said: " . . . O Lord, I yield unto Thy will, and joyfully embrace that sorrow thou wilt have me suffer. . . . Let calamity be the exerc ise, but not the overthrow of my virtue." '[5]

Milton need not have been anxious. Sidney's *Arcadia* was neither vain nor merely amatorious, Charles's reading in it before his beheading neither frivolous nor misdirected. It was a book, in fact, intended for the instruction in virtue and in the art of government of princes and gentlemen, in prosperity and adversity, limning out exact pictures of every posture in the mind.

In spite of its title and its reputation the elements of Romance and Pastoral in the *Arcadia* are not of primary importance. The pastoral setting is merely decorative. Confined mainly to the eclogues with which each book ends, it amounts to little more than a series of poetic interludes. Loosely attached to the main story, these occasionally supply a vaguely pertinent comment on some aspect of Love-and-Fortune required by the plot. Similarly with the Romance furniture: there are Greek names in abundance, variegated love-stories and complicated adventures; storms at sea, and rescues from pirates; oracles of Delphi, and miraculous salves to restore blistered beauty; resuscitations of the seeming dead, and maidens who follow their lovers disguised as squires; jewels and birthmarks, evil queens, marauding bears—almost everything, in external detail, that appears in Shakespeare's last plays. But as with Shakespeare so with Sidney. The difference between Greene's *Pandosto* and *A Winter's Tale* is the difference a mature and practised philosophy makes. Sidney's *Arcadia*, too, has the largeness of an erected wit, 'that second nature, which in nothing he sheweth so much as in Poetrie'.

It is of the seriousness of Sidney's 'erected wit' we are most aware in reading the *Arcadia*. Its pattern imposes itself throughout. There is, for example, the shipwreck with which the book starts. Musidorus, washed ashore and separated from his friend, goes back with a shepherd and a fisherman to what appears to be the wreck of a burning ship:

'They steered therefore as near thitherward as they could: but when they came so near that their eyes were full masters of the object, they saw a sight full of piteous strangeness: a ship, or rather the carcase of a ship, or rather some few bones of the carcase hulling there, part broken, part burned, part drowned: death having used more than one dart to that destruction. And amidst the precious things were a number of dead bodies, which likewise did not only testify both elements' violence, but that the chief violence was grown of human inhumanity: for their bodies were full of grisly wounds, and their blood had (as it were) filled the wrinkles of the sea's visage; which it seemed the sea would not wash away that it might witness that it is not always its fault when we do condemn its cruelty. In sum, a defeat where the conquered kept both field and spoil; a shipwreck without storm or ill-footing; and a waste of fire in the midst of the water.'[6]

This is the end of the Princes' voyage over the sea of Fortune, 'when the conspired heavens had gotten this subject of their wrath upon so fit a place as the sea was'. It is a sea gravely and appropriately moralized. The writer's eye is master of the object, and he sees with his mind. The pattern imposed is not an external formalism. 'A ship, or rather the carcase of a ship, or rather some few bones of the carcase hulling there, part broken, part burned, part drowned: death having used more than one dart to that destruction': the ship becomes a stricken animal, yet the broken, charred, and half-submerged ribs are vividly kept before us as those of an actual galleon awash and about to sink; the personification of death is not an inert trope, and the conventional darts are forgotten in the carefully prepared-for suggestion of what Malory would call the mort of a beast. At the same time 'broken . . . burned . . . drowned' points to a significant progression in violence—human passion, human heedlessness, and finally the engulfing elemental these have made a way for: 'the chief violence was grown of human inhumanity.' Blood lay in the troughs of the ruffled sea: but such a paraphrase misses the real force of Sidney's image:

'blood had (as it were) filled the wrinkles of the sea's visage; which it seemed the sea would not wash away, that it might witness that it is not always its fault when we do condemn its cruelty.'

Sidney makes the sea a vivid face—an aged, suffering, fallen, and outraged nature; yet he remembers too the right order of things—the dignity of man whereby he is free to sin, the dignity of his first responsibility to himself and to God.

In his *Apologie* Sidney criticized the mere historian as one 'yet better knowing how this world goeth, than how his own wit runneth'.[7] The poet, he claimed, would be the man capable of knowing both the worlds, that of external event and that of inner motive and meaning. Shipwrecks, romantic encounters, accidental turns abound in the *Arcadia*. They are a part of the province of Fortune. Sidney, however, was more interested still in the inner environment of man—with the war in his own members. We can conveniently illustrate this by a further quotation. Musidorus has finally met his friend Pyrocles (who was not, as he thought, destroyed in the shipwreck) only to be confronted with a startling change in him: Pyrocles is in love, and has left him. 'Ah,' Musidorus exclaims,

'Pyrocles, what means this alteration? What have I deserved of thee to be thus banished of thy counsels? Heretofore I have accused the sea, condemned the pirates, and hated my evil fortune that deprived me of thee; but now thyself is the sea which drowns my comfort; thyself is the pirate that robs thyself from me; thy own will becomes thy evil fortune.'[8]

The macrocosm is reflected in the microcosm. Sidney is only concerned to bring the two together, as neither the mere romance nor the purely pastoral does. There is Fortune and there is Virtue.

The shipwreck description is not one of Sidney's purple patches. And as we have seen the pattern it reveals is not an arbitrary or conventional one imposed from the outside. It is the imprint of a mind mastering its objects. Sidney's style is balanced, antithetical, alliterative, calculated. At its most typical, however, it is always an instrument for the 'erected wit'—for the analysis such a wit must make, and for the rapid but considered juxtapositions such a wit will also drive towards; analysis of the separate conflicting parts, juxtaposition of the two worlds in synthesis. Sidney saw the world in terms of division, balance, and resolution. His style is a reflection of his vision.

What is apparent in detail, is also obvious on the larger scale. The whole *Arcadia* is organized on a basis of contrasts and complements, not pedantically, but sufficiently to give the strength of structural relevance to the main incidents as they occur, and to the various sub-plots that are woven into it. The two exemplars of ideal manhood are balanced by two perfect women. The women are studies in what might appear as a Sidneian version of Sense and Sensibility. The princes, in the same way, are poised one against the other. Musidorus is the more manly yet the less beautiful; Pyrocles, 'a Mars' heart in a Cupid's body', combines man and woman's excellence in himself, yet is betrayed once at least by his oversensitivity.... And so on. The sense of grouping and shape in the *Arcadia* makes it a unity rather than a conglomerate, intricately winding as its events and stories are.

The external world, from one point of view, is the sphere of the heroical; the internal the sphere of what Milton called the amatorious. In the one are required the active virtues of courage, mental fortitude, command over men and events; in the other the passive and maybe unrewarded virtues—singleness, self-devotion, command over one's will and one's possible self-division. Each is a school of virtue. Both came within the orbit of the larger and inclusive qualities which Pamela exemplifies in her prayer, and which Sidney, mindful of the educated Christian tradition in which he was writing, indicates when he couples 'patience' with Aristotle's 'magnanimitie'. Adversity is the supreme test of human quality. A Romance is an account of adversity successfully endured. Patience and magnanimity, after the storm and other hard plights, are then seen to 'shine the more in the neere-following prosperitie'.

There are, then, the two separate but related spheres in the Sidneain universe. One is the outer world of public events, the other the inner world of private affections. One is heroical, the other amatorious. One is the sphere of magnanimity, the other the sphere for the exercise of patience. More notably still, one is the especially masculine world, the other the world in which the womanly nature finds its supreme expression. The counterpoise is marked, pattern is emphasized throughout, but there is no meretricious artifice. The *Arcadia* is Sidney's greatest synthesis. His intention is to be serious and all-embracing, to offer a coherent and compendious view of life. Patience and magnanimity, like man and woman, are opposite and yet complementary. The supreme perfection will be the marriage of the two. From the nature of things, however, the marriage will not be possible in a single character. The single character will be man or woman, in need all the time of his complement—another person. Perfection will be a co-operative rather than an individual achievement. Thus friendship and love are of central importance, as well as the notion of society—the ordered unity of distinct parts. The 'sly enemy that doth most separate a man from well-doing' is solitariness. Both Stoicism and Platonism are radically transformed by Sidney's renaissance Christianization. His vision of perfection is opposed to any idea of the humanly self-sufficient. It is rather to be found expressed in such a scene as the Messenger saw when he came to the palace of Parthenia and Argalus. Parthenia and Argalus are the Phoenix and the Turtle of the *Arcadia*:

'The messenger made speed, and found Argalus at a castle of his own, sitting in a parlour with the fair Parthenia, he reading in a book the stories of Hercules, she by him as to hear him read: but while his eyes looked on the book, she looked in his eyes, and sometimes staying him with some petty question, not so much to be resolved of the doubt, as to give him occasion to look upon her: a happy couple, he joying in her, she joying in herself, but in herself because she enjoyed him: both increased their riches by giving to each other; each making one life double, because they made a double life one; where desire never wanted satisfaction, nor satisfaction ever bred satiety; he ruling because she would obey, or rather because she would obey, he there ruling in.'[9]

Such moments as these are the reward of virtue, of the fight against the evil that arises from passion both in the external world of action and in the private world of love. Virtue pervades both the fields of patience and magnanimity. However, though such moments are possible they can be guaranteed no permanence. The messenger, for example, is arriving at the palace of Argalus with a request for help against Amphialus, who holds the princesses prisoner. Out of loyalty Argalus will answer the call on him, will fight Amphialus, and will be killed. Parthenia likewise, on hearing of her husband's death, will disguise herself in armour, herself challenge Amphialus to mortal combat, and she too will die. The universe pervaded by the possibilities of Virtue is also subjected to all the contingencies of Fortune. Virtue and Fortune, too, are opposites that need each other. Virtue is a successful but precarious command over events and over one's self. It is a temporary balance in the midst of tensions. The tensions constantly change, and constantly threaten the stability maintained by commanding them. Magnanimity is Virtue in its aspect of successful command: when Fortune is compelled to be the well-waiting handmaid. Patience is Virtue in its aspect of sufferance rather than control: when Fortune is frowning. Both virtues are necessary. The adversity we must fight against and the adversity we must submit to come from God. In 'a storm or in other hard plights' we are not only tested but we are also tempered. In good fortune or in bad, we need to centre our mind on that which is above the flux; in the one case to avoid over-weening pride, in the other to avoid the dangerous defeatism of despair. Such is the large frame in which Sidney's romantic-pastoral is set. It is something gravely moral, Christian, and renaissance, in spite of its Greek names and pre-Christian terminology; something which impressed Sidney's contemporaries, fortified Charles in his final days, and led Sir William Temple at the end of the century to write:

'The true Spirit or Vein of Ancient Poetry, in this kind, seems to shine most in Sir Philip Sidney, whom I esteem both the greatest Poet and Noblest Genius of any that have left Writings behind them, and published in ours or any other modern Language.'[10]

* * *

The *Arcadia* does not begin at the beginning. It opens with the shipwreck scene, already quoted, and the stranding of Musidorus —one of the heroes—on the shores of Arcadia. What has preceded this is told retrospectively in Book II. Book I has to present the large themes of the romance, or a part of them, and bring us quickly into touch not only with the princes but also with the princesses. For the action concerns the two worlds and the two parties.

Musidorus, within the bounds of his humanity, and with the limitations Sidney recognizes as attaching to all the virtues, is ideal:

'besides his bodily gifts beyond the degree of admiration . . . a mind of most excellent composition, a piercing wit, quite void of ostentation, high erected thought seated in a heart of courtesy, an eloquence as sweet in the uttering as slow to come to the uttering, a behaviour so noble as gave a majesty to adversity; and all this in a man whose age could not be above one and twenty years.'[11]

Musidorus is taken to the house of Kalander, the King's brother, a subject but we also feel a peer. It is here that we get the picture of what is clearly recognizable as the Elizabethan Great House, the Wilton or Penshurst. Kalander explains to Musidorus the situation with regard to his brother, the King. Basilius has consulted the oracle at Delphi, and the oracle has ambiguously prophesied dire consequences to follow on his daughter's marriage. To prevent this fate Basilius has gone into complete retirement with his family, cutting off himself from governmental responsibility, and his daughters from all society. The Great House comments adversely on the King's conduct. Both Kalander and the Vice-regent disapprove. Basilius, in fact, in running away from his fate is showing himself incapable of either patience or magnanimity. He is in this the foil for Musidorus and Pyrocles. He is doing his duty neither by himself, his family, nor his country. More than this, it is made clear that his 'judgement' has been thoroughly 'corrupted with a prince's fortune'. Forgetting that 'his office is not to make men, but to use men as they are', he has preferred a clown to the place of chief favourite and given his elder daughter into his keeping. 'But truly', Kalander drily remarks, 'so it is that princes (whose doings have been often smoothed with good success) think nothing so absurd, which they cannot make honourable.'[12]

Musidorus must be joined with his friend Pyrocles. The reunion is effected by a rebellion of the Helots, the dispossessed of a neighbouring state, who are now rising against their oppressors. The friends find themselves heading the opposite parties (as if the accidents of political faction arise by chance in the field of Fortune and cut across Virtue as a considered choice). They fight, recognize each other, and compose the quarrel. So that Musidorus and Pyrocles are together again, and both of them enjoying Kalander's hospitality. The episode of the Helot's rising is the last of their unambiguous adventures in the world of external actions. For almost as soon as they are returned to Kalander's Great House Pyrocles sees a portrait of the Princess Philoclea, Basilius' younger daughter, and is obviously falling in love.

The first sign of his new condition is that he withdraws from the society of Kalander's castle. Nor is the hitherto unshakeable campaign loyalty of friendship able to make the company of Musidorus preferable to solitude. Musidorus, however, seeks out his friend and a long debate ensues—the first of several in the *Arcadia*. In this instance the discussion turns upon the heroic life of active virtue, and the apparently contemplative withdrawal from the world to which Pyrocles is now committing himself. Against the 'sly enemy' of solitariness Musidorus argues 'in the praise of honourable action',

'in showing that such a kind of contemplation is but a glorious title to idleness; that in action a man did not only better himself but benefit others . . . that the mind should best know his own good or evil by practice; which knowledge was the only way to increase the one, and correct the other.'[13]

There is something Miltonic in Musidorus. Pyrocles has at this point no effective reply, except to insist that the 'knowledges' Musidorus praises,

'as they are of good use, so are they not all the mind may stretch itself to: who knows whether I feed not my mind with higher thoughts?'[14]

Pyrocles' real reply comes later—when he has secretly left Kalander's and insinuated himself into the household of Basilius. There Musidorus finds him disguised as an Amazon and radiant with Belphoebe-like beauty. Musidorus now realizes that the enemy is not solitariness but love, and, not having proved its power yet himself, is hard on 'this effeminate love' which 'doth so womanize a man'. Pyrocles, however, can now speak firmly on behalf of a mode of virtue which is higher than the heroic, while still including it. His defence necessitates a defence of woman:

'I am not yet come to that degree of wisdom to think light of the sex of whom I have my life, since if I be anything, which your friendship rather finds than I acknowledge, I was, to come to it, born of a woman, and nursed of a woman. And certainly . . . it is strange to see the unmanlike cruelty of mankind, who, not content with their tyrannous ambitions to have brought the others' virtuous patience under them, like childish masters, think their masterhood nothing without doing injury to them, who, if we will argue by reason, are framed by nature with the same parts of the mind for the exercise of virtue as we are.'[15]

And of love as the response of one virtue to another:

'For those kinds of bitter objections as that lust, idleness, and a weak heart should be, as it were, the matter and form of love, rather touch me, Musidorus, than love; but I am good witness of my own imperfections, and therefore will not defend myself: but herein I must say you deal contrary to yourself: for if I be so weak, then can you not with reason stir me up as you did by remembrance of my own virtue; or if indeed I be virtuous, then must ye confess that love hath his working in a virtuous heart; and so no doubt hath it, whatsoever I be: for, if we love virtue, in whom shall we love it but in a virtuous creature? without your meaning be, I should love this word Virtue, where I see it written in a book.'[16]

Though Pyrocles' disguise is necessitated by the plot (Basilius will not permit men to enter his retreat) it can also be seen as a touch of Sidneian allegory. Pyrocles, 'a Mars's heart in a Cupid's body', 'the uttermost that in mankind might be seen', asserts the feminine also. His dress adds to rather than diminishes his merely masculine virtue. Throughout the story it is Sidney's intention to make Pyrocles the dominant figure. His women, though they might sometimes wear armour, never do so in fact with the success of Spenser's Belphoebe. In Pyrocles, however, he would seem to be insisting that man is capable of a synthesis of qualities that includes the womanly yet avoids the hermaphroditic. The merely masculine prowess Musidorus argues for is a lesser thing than this: as Musidorus discovers when he in his turn submits to love in the person of Pamela—Basilius' elder daughter.

The implicit moralization of Pyrocles' costume serves an important purpose at this point in the story. It is because of what it *means* that the transvestism is not offensive. The meaning, too, prevents the confusion of our sympathies that would otherwise arise as the plot proceeds. Because Pyrocles as a woman has to be the object of Basilius' irregular passion, and Pyrocles as a man has similarly to be pursued by Basilius' wife. And the Princess Philoclea will first innocently fall in love with him as a woman, and, when she discovers his true identity, find herself in easy transit to a full sexual love-relation with him. Without Sidney's gravely beautiful handling of Pyrocles' dual nature at this point, the ensuing tangle would be either impossibly ridiculous or obscene. The plot needs to be kept in closest touch with the meanings Sidney is careful to infuse into it. When this is done, increments of fuller significance attach to the separate incidents. Basilius' conduct, for example, becomes then the expression of a nature fallen below manhood—of a 'womanized man' whose behaviour inside his retreat is strictly of a piece with the already effeminate defeatism his flight from Fortune clearly declares.

The courses of the two love-affairs of the princes and princesses are as carefully patterned as the comparisons and parallels between the persons themselves. There is so much deliberate design in the book that we may be tempted to push the meanings too far. Sidney, however, is so consciously the intellectual moralizer of his material that in any case where we might suspect discrepancy, it is wise to bear in mind the possibility that we have missed his plan. What might seem his confusion might be our obtuseness. The placing of the two pairs of lovers in relation to each other and to the moral scheme of the book is a case in point.

Of the two princes it is Pyrocles who seems intended for the leading role: while both are excellent, he is pre-excellent. The two princesses are similarly discriminated. Yet Pyrocles falls in love with Philoclea, the younger and softer-natured; and Musidorus with Pamela. And, in the eventual imprisonment episode, it is Pamela who dominates, not Philoclea. And, in the conduct of the love-affairs, it is Pamela who demonstrates most clearly that women 'are framed by nature with the same parts of the mind for the exercise of virtue' as men are. Pamela seems to synthesize women-and-man, as Pyrocles combines man-and-woman. Yet Sidney pairs them off in a way that does not appear to fall in with the requirements of the logical pattern. Before pressing any thesis, it might be wise to look at Sidney's own definitions. We suggested that Pamela and Philoclea were Sense and Sensibility. This is too crude a formula to cover precisely what Sidney intends. Kalander describes them as follows:

'The elder is named Pamela; by many men not deemed inferior to her sister: for my part, when I marked them both, methought there was (if at least such perfections may receive the word of more) more sweetness in Philoclea but more majesty in Pamela: methought love played in Philoclea's eyes, and threatened in Pamela's; methought Philoclea's beauty only persuaded, but so persuaded as all hearts must yield; Pamela's beauty used violence, and such violence as no heart could resist. And it seems that such proportion is between their minds; Philoclea so bashful, as though her excellencies had stolen into her before she was aware; so humble that she will put all pride out of countenance; in sum, such proceedings as will stir hope but teach hope good manners. Pamela of high thoughts who avoids not pride with not knowing her excellencies, but by making that one of her excellencies to be void of pride; her mother's wisdom, greatness, nobility, but (if I can guess aright) knit with a more constant temper.'[17]

Part of our difficulty here might be that Sidney's discriminations are finer than we have been in the habit of making for three hundred years. The two princesses are put side by side and differentiated. Yet Sidney deprecates any subordination of one to the other. The method of presentation seems comparative, yet comparison is not entirely Sidney's aim: the sisters do not occupy positions on a scale that makes comparison possible. Nor is contrast part of the intention, though the pair are so unlike as to seem poles apart. Each princess is herself a perfection. Nothing could add to either. They are not complementary to one another, for that would argue their mutual incompleteness. And yet when we have said all this there is still the overruling impression of one's being weighed against the other, the sense of scrupulous and fine assessment that saves the passage from becoming merely hyperbole. The main distinction between them is, it would seem, that Pamela's is a conscious and deliberately maintained virtue, Philoclea's a perfection of nature in which instinctive rightness of constitution effects the same as a properly directed will. Pamela would not depart from virtue, Philoclea could not. The desire *not* to compare or contrast, or to consider the sisters as complementary, comes from Sidney's unwillingness to make a doctrinaire decision—a choice which would in a case like this be an impoverishment: the choice Wordsworth too refrained from making when he turned in his sonnet from himself, the conscious devotee of the Mighty Being, to the 'dear child' at his side, who lay in Abraham's bosom all the year, God being with her when even Wordsworth knew it not. Philoclea is Sidney's version of what the Romantics thought of as instinctive virtue:

'The sweet minded Philoclea was in their degree of well-doing, to whom the not knowing of evil serveth for a ground of virtue, and hold their inward powers in better form with an unspotted simplicity, than many who rather cunningly seek to know what goodness is than willingly take into themselves the following of it. But as that sweet and simple breath of heavenly goodness is the easier to be altered because it hath not passed through the worldly wickedness, nor feelingly found the evil that evil carries with it, so now the lady Philoclea (whose eyes and senses had received nothing, but according as the natural course of each thing required; whose tender youth had obediently lived under her parents' behests, without framing out of her own will the fore-choosing of any thing) when now she came to a point wherein her judgment was to be practised in knowing faultiness by his first tokens, she was like a young fawn who, coming in the wind of the hunters, doth now know whether it be a thing or not to be eschewed; whereof at this time she began to get a costly experience.'[18]

Where each of the four lovers wears a halo, the modern reader can be expected to suffer some of the dazzle and confusion of excessive bright. Still, Sidney seems to have been sure of the distinctions he was making, and clear as to what his design should convey. Musidorus might have been assailable only by the sort of beauty which used violence, by a majesty in woman which united wisdom, greatness, nobility, and a masculine consciousness equal to the domination of any circumstance: a combination of rigorous intellect and strenuous will. Pamela, the woman who has a man's mind, might be expected to respond only to the purely masculine when she meets it—in a Musidorus retailing the story of his heroic deeds as a means of gaining access to his mistress' heart; a man whose natural element was battle, his dress the armour of virtue tempered in external conflict. Similarly, the man Pyrocles, who also transcends the merely male, might be predestinate for the essence of pure femininity incarnated in Philoclea. Alternatively, if we accept the notion of some qualitative difference between the two princes and the two princesses, Musidorus and Pamela might be seen to be united through the conscious and willed virtue they have in common; Pyrocles' and Philoclea's may be a still higher marriage—a mating effective at the point where reason and nature coalesce in love. The union is suggestive of the Phoenix and the Turtle: a reason above reason find its counterpart in a perfection reason could adore but never construct.

The courses of the lovers' courtship are also in balance against each other. The difference between the two can most clearly be seen in terms of the conduct of the princesses. It is with them that the initiative lies. Philoclea grows naturally into love, through what she at first thinks is a woman's friendship for a woman. Pamela's love is a series of deliberate steps and considered choices. With her, Musidorus must 'taste the grain of rigour delightedly'. And of the two princes it is Musidorus who breaks the code which, in Pyrocles, is not so much as felt to be a code but rather a harmonious decorum—not a curb or a frustration but the natural form which instinctive delight requires for its own expression and fulfilment. Of the two princesses, therefore, it is Pamela who has to inflict the disciplinary rebuke. Musidorus kisses her before she has given permission. Her anger precipitates him into remorse, and he banishes himself from her presence.

The banishment serves the purpose also of the story. While Musidorus is away Pyrocles (still in disguise) and the two princesses are decoyed to the castle of Cecropia. Cecropia is the queen-villain of the *Arcadia*, something like Lady Macbeth and something like the queen in *Cymbeline*: ambitious, envious, passionately material, and her son's evil genius. Her son Amphialus is also in love with Philoclea. He is no party to the plot to capture the princesses, but accepts the captivity once it is an accomplished fact. Amphialus is a noble nature, but overswayed by his mother and by events. His error is twofold. His one-sided passion blinds him to the impersonal grounding of love in virtue. He imagines that a substitute for this can be supplied by a marriage based on duress and the dictates of Fortune. The capture of the princesses was none of his devising, but he will try now to make use of it. He misconceives, of course, in this, the nature of both love and virtue. He underrates the peculiar strengths which are inherent in woman. He commits himself to a course which will lead rapidly from passive consent in an initial wrong committed by another on his behalf to deliberate and wilful wrongdoing on his own initiative. For his castle is attacked. Amphialus has to defend it with all the means he can devise. He calls a muster-roll of rebellion and summons to him all the accumulated discontents of Basilius' kingdom. In Sidney's account of Amphialus' preparations there is an inclusive breadth of view and depth of insight into man as a political animal:

'First, he dispatched private letters to all those principal lords and gentlemen of the country whom he thought either alliance, or friendship to himself, might draw with special motion from the general consideration of duty: not omitting all such, whom either youthful age, or youthlike minds did fill with unlimited desires: besides such whom any discontentment made hungry of change, or an overspended want made want a civil war: to each (according to the counsel of his mother) conforming himself after their humours. To his friend, friendliness; to the ambitious, great expectations; to the displeased, revenge; to the greedy, spoil; wrapping their hopes with such cunning that they rather seemed given over unto them as partakers, than promises sprung of necessity. . . . But because he knew how violently rumours do blow the sails of popular judgments, and how few there be that can discern between truth and truth-likeness, between shows and substance, he caused a justification of his action to be written, whereof were sowed abroad many copies, which with some glosses of probability, might hide indeed the foulness of his treason; and from true commonplaces, fetch down most false applications. For beginning in how much the duty which is owed to the country, goes beyond all other duties, since in itself it contains them all; and that for the respect thereof, not only all tender respects of kindred, or whatsoever other friendships, are to be laid aside, but that even long-held opinions (rather builded upon a secret of government than any ground of truth) are to be forsaken; he fell by degrees to show that since the end whereto anything is directed is ever of more noble reckoning, than the thing whereto directed, that therefore the weal-public was more to be regarded than any person or magistrate that thereunto was ordained.' [19]

Amphialus is no crude rebel and machiavel. Sidney, in fact, esteems his outstanding qualities as man, soldier, and politician. Yet Amphialus can use truth-likeness instead of truth as successfully as Shakespeare's Richard III or Edmund. But there is no overstraining of the credible. On the contrary, the portrait brings convincingly before us the high strategic grasp of the renaissance man of state affairs, of the international diplomat such as Sidney was himself. It is only when we see Amphialus that we can appreciate how raw an Elizabethan Shakespeare is —how distant he is from education in the real world of revolt and dynastic strain which Sidney knew from the inside. Amphialus is the main agent of misfortune in the book. His defection is the chief cause of the princesses' distress. Yet he is not drawn as a renegade. Rather, he is a study in virtue which just fails of its true centre, and which becomes thereby more dangerous than open and avowed malice. He is goodness becoming by default the tool-villain.

The imprisonment of the princesses is their great testing time. Again, Amphialus is not implicated directly in the torments they undergo. His mother, however, has her own methods and her own views on how to handle the prisoners. Philoclea and Pamela are submitted first to reasoned persuasion and finally to torture both mental and physical. The captivity episode portray their heroism in the sphere where only patience can be operative—the woman's virtue—just as the episodes that have led up to it have Musidorus and Pyrocles as their heroes and portrays the masculine qualities of heroic magnanimity, courage, endurance, and command.

Cecropia plies each of the sisters in turn. And again, throughout Book III, Philoclea and Pamela are poised against each other in the equal Sidneian scales. Philoclea is described in adversity in words that recall the Gentleman's account of Cordelia receiving the news of her father's distress:

'sitting low upon a cushion in such a given-over manner, that one would have thought silence, solitariness and melancholy were come there under the ensign of mishap, to conquer delight, and drive him from his natural state of beauty: her tears came dropping down like rain in sunshine, and she not taking heed to wipe her tears, they hung upon her cheeks and lips as upon cherries which the dropping tree bedeweth. In the dressing of her hair and apparel, she might see neither a careful art, nor an art of carelessness, but even left to neglected chance, which yet could no more imperfect her perfections than a die any way cast could lose its squareness.'[20]

Sidney's last phrase is illuminating. Adversity can only add new perfection to the old in a person centred in the 'second nature' of virtue. Cecropia cannot understand this. She is a merely natural woman of unerected wit. She weighs 'Philoclea's resolutions by the counterpoise of her own youthful thoughts'. An 'unexpert virgin' must at once respond to flattery, the prospect of a good marriage, and release from imprisonment. Cecropia wears at first 'a vizard of kindness'. Her promises sound seductive:

'The way I will show you; which if it be not the gate builded hitherto in your private choice, yet shall be a door to bring you through a garden of pleasures, as sweet as this life can bring forth; nay rather, which makes this life to be a life.'[21]

The picture of Cecropia, like that of Amphialus, is not overdrawn. Cecropia becomes sinister only when her words echo, as they do, in the context of the higher ethic and the deeper spiritual insight which Sidney incarnates in his heroine. Pleasures do not make this life to be a life. Adversity has a positive role when it is met with steadfastness. Philoclea remains unmoved. She

'heard some pieces of her speeches, not otherwise than one doth when a tedious prattler cumbers the hearing of a delightful music'.[22]

There is neither contempt nor anger in her reaction, yet her remove above Cecropia is given delicate emphasis. She simply belongs to another world, to the delightful music of which she is attuned. And, like Cordelia, in this world she is a queen.

Cecropia then turns to Pamela, whom she finds walking up and down 'full of deep though patient thoughts', composing her mind to the prayer Charles I was later to read. Where Philoclea avoided Cecropia's assaults 'with sweet and humble dealing', Pamela beats them off 'with the majesty of virtue'. Cecropia first attempts flattery: Pamela's beauty is such that it will give her absolute power over men. Pamela takes the compliment lightly: beauty 'ought to be held in dearness according to the excellency, and no more than we would do of things which we account precious, never to suffer it to be defiled'. Defilement, of course, is the last thing that Cecropia would wish: rather, fulfilment, the joining of beauty to love and youth to delight. Pamela is still not affected. She plays the role of dutiful daughter (a role she deliberately casts aside later, when she decides to go off with Musidorus): Amphialus must first get her father's consent to marriage before he can hope to obtain hers. Cecropia then attacks the idea of filial obedience, especially when the parents are peevish. Finally the citadel of Pamela's steadfastness is attacked. Cecropia puts forward the arguments of the civilized atheist (educated in the heathen classics and in Machiavelli) to undermine the basis of Pamela's faith.[23] Her speech foreshadows *Lear* in more than its references to Thunder and to 'flies':[24]

'For as children must first by fear be induced to know that which after when they do know, they are most glad of, so are these bugbears of opinions brought by great clerks into the world to serve as shields to keep them from those faults, whereto else the vanity of the world, and weakness of senses might pull them. But in you, niece, whose excellency is such as it need not be held up by the staff of vulgar opinions, I would not you should love virtue servilely, for fear of I know not what, which you see not, but even for the good effects of virtue which you see. Fear, and indeed foolish fear, and fearful ignorance, was the first inventor of those conceits; for when they heard it thunder, not knowing the natural cause, they thought there was some angry body above that spake so loud: and ever the less they did perceive, the more they did conceive; whereof they knew no cause, that grew straight a miracle: foolish folks not marking that the alterations be but upon particular accidents, and universality being always one. Yesterday was but as today, and tomorrow will tread the same footsteps of his foregoers: so as it is manifest enough that all things follow but the course of their own nature, saving only man, who while by the pregnancy of his imagination he strives to things supernatural, meanwhile he loseth his own natural felicity. Be wise, and that wisdom shall be a God unto thee; be contented, and that is thy heaven; for else to think that those powers, if there be any such, above are moved either by the eloquence of our prayers, or in a chafe at the folly of our actions, carries as much reason, as if flies should think that men take great care which of them hums sweetest, and which of them flies nimblest.'[25]

Pamela, however, is well able to contain the attack. She meets Cecropia on her own ground, and demolishes her arguments one by one. Evil in the *Arcadia* is also Error, known to be such, and shown to be such, not a Conradian Incomprehensible that arouses nameless and benumbing fear. Without being robbed of its due force, without being minimized or rationalized away, the irrational of Evil, like the irrational of Beauty itself, is estimated in accordance with its quality. It is an error of the mind and of the will. Both errors the erected wit can comprehend and avoid. Sidney's gravity, certainty, and serenity of tone, rest on this act of comprehension, this combination of intellect and experience.

Cecropia is defeated by 'disdain in the one, and patience in the other'—'silence and patience (like a fair gorgeous armour, hammered upon by an ill-favoured smith)'. There is a third prisoner, however—Pyrocles himself—and in him we see patience defective. One of Cecropia's last tricks is to arrange a mock beheading of Philoclea which Pyrocles witnesses from his window. Pyrocles falls short of the ideal in the way he reacts to this final thrust of Fortune. It is maybe because he is a man. It is maybe, too, a possibly unresolved clash in Sidney's mind—a slight hesitation—between the two ethical systems he is trying to harmonize: the system of Christian sufferance under the worst blows that can befall, and the system of neo-Chivalric Love which requires that Love also should be an absolute. In any event, Pyrocles—like Lear—questions the rightness of the whole scheme of things:

'It was not pity, it was not amasement, it was not a sorrow which then laid hold of Pyrocles, but a wild fury of desperate agony: so that he cried out, "O tyrant heaven, traitor earth, blind providence, no justice, how is this done? how is this suffered? hath this world a government? if it have, let it pour out all its mischiefs upon me, and see whether it have power to make me more wretched than I am. Did she excel for this? have I prayed for this? abominable hand that did it; detestable devil that commanded it; cursed light that beheld it; and if the light be cursed, what then are mine eyes that have seen it? and have I seen Philoclea dead, and do I live? and do I live not to help her, but to talk to her? and stand I still talking?" and with that, carried by the madness of anguish, not having a readier way to kill himself, he ran as hard as ever he could with his head against the wall, with intention to brain himself. . . .'[26]

Suicide in the *Arcadia* is an extreme falling-away from the frame of patience—a final sin. Pyrocles' attempt is unsuccessful. When he comes to he hears a voice crying 'Revenge, Revenge,' and his bloody-minded resolve to 'destroy man, woman, and child' in any way connected with the castle is noted as at least an improvement on blank despair. Suicide—the very worst of fates—is reserved for Cecropia herself, when her attempts are finally proved futile, and Amphialus discovers them, and comes running towards his mother with a drawn sword in his hand.

Sidney's revision of the *Arcadia* goes only a little further than this. And, indeed, having reached this point he had covered the main inner territories of his story—the two spheres of 'patience and magnanimitie'; the spheres of womanly and manly excellence, the spiritual and the political, and the ethic of the Arcadian love-relationship in which these two are significantly brought together. Sidney's original plan, however, allowed for one further great turn to his theme.

The princesses are rescued from Amphialus's castle, by Pyrocles fighting their would-be ravishers on the inside and by Musidorus simultaneously breaking the castle's defences from the outside. The four lovers return to Basilius's lodge. Musidorus and Pamela make their escape together. Pyrocles and Philoclea are just ready to effect theirs when they are discovered. Unfortunately, Basilius (who has been tricked into sleeping with his own wife instead of with his hoped-for Amazon, Pyrocles) has also taken a love-potion which produces a death-like trance. Alarm spreads through the realm. The four lovers (Musidorus and Pamela too are recaptured) have to stand trial. Their judge is Euarchus—a visiting monarch, actually the father of Pyrocles, and an ideally just ruler. The princes are to be tried for bringing about the King's death and for intending to marry the heirs to the throne without parental consent. It has been suggested, and it might be, that this is the confrontation of the new ethic of love with the older traditional ethic of filial obedience, the weighing of the demands of the private world of virtue against the demands of the public world of security.[27] The judgment goes against Pyrocles and Musidorus. The father condemns his son for the offence, and a tragic ending is only avoided by Basilius's startling 'resurrection'.

What is Sidney's intention in the last part of his romance—so given over to the collapse of the lovers' schemes and their trial and condemnation? There is no doubt of the sustained seriousness with which the story continues. Sidney does not lose interest in this theme. He conducts it still in such a manner as he ascribes to Euarchus himself, 'with that well-poised gesture unpassionate nature bestoweth upon mankind'. It has been suggested that the trial-scene reveals an unresolved conflict of the two ethics. It is possible, however, to view Sidney's ending in another light.

Pyrocles while captive in the castle with the two princesses had been tempted to commit suicide. On this occasion his mind had been overthrown by despair: he had just witnessed, as he thought, Philoclea's execution. His second captivity has a different setting. It is a legal imprisonment according to the law of the country. The circumstances of his second temptation are likewise different from the first. Now he wishes to take his life in order to save Philoclea from disgrace. Suicide will be the expression of love, honour, selflessness, and virtue: 'this my doing is out of judgment, not sprung from passion.' Philoclea has to dissuade him, and Sidney gives as much importance to the argument here as he gave to that between Pamela and Cecropia on the nature of the universe:

' "And if we be lieutenants of God in this little castle, do you not think we must take warning of Him to give over our charge when He leaves us unprovided of good means to tarry in it?" "No certainly do I not," answered the sorrowful Philoclea, "since it is not for us to appoint that mighty majesty what time He will help us; the uttermost instant is scope enough for Him to revoke everything to one's desire. And therefore to prejudicate His determination is but a doubt of goodness in Him who is nothing but goodness. But when indeed He doth either by sickness, or outward force lay death upon us, then are we to take knowledge that such is His pleasure, and to know that all is well that He doth. That we should be masters of ourselves, we can show it at all no title or claim; since neither we made ourselves, nor bought ourselves, we can stand upon no other right by His gift, which he must limit as it pleaseth Him." '[28]

Suicide, Philoclea argues, 'hath not his ground in an assured virtue', but 'proceeds rather of some other disguised passion'. Finally, Pyrocles submits to her wisdom.

Thus the princes learn patience, too, in this last trial of manhood and add a further (and Christian) virtue to 'magnanimitie'. They conduct themselves in their captivity 'like men indeed, fortifying courage with the true rampire of patience, (and) did so endure that they did rather appear governors of necessity, than servants of fortune'.[29] They are reconciled to death, the last affliction. They sing a hymn which falls naturally into its place at this moment when the full pressure of Sidney's Christian purpose is felt to be weighing on the heroical-pastoral-romance, giving it the full imprint of his protestant seriousness:

Since nature's works be good, and death doth serve
As nature's work: why should we fear to die?
Since fear is vain, but when it may preserve:
Why should we fear that which we cannot fly?

Fear is more pain than is the pain it fears,
Disarming human minds of native might:
While each conceit an ugly figure bears,
Which were not evil well view'd in reason's light.

Our owly eyes, which dimm'd with passions be,
And scarce discern the dawn of coming day,
Let them be clear'd, and now begin to see,
Our life is but a step in dusty way.

Then let us hold the bliss of peaceful mind,
Since this we feel, great loss we cannot find.[30]

And Sidney's comment reads almost like a re-echo of his *Apologie* when defending the story of Ulysses:

'Thus did they, like quiet swans, sing their own obsequies, and virtuously enable their minds against all extremities which they did think would fall upon them.'

Part of Sidney's intention, it would thus appear, is to bring the ethic of love within a wider scheme. It is not merely put in opposition to what Euarchus, the perfect governor, stands for.

Rather, it is subordinated to Fortune—a last and exciting turn in Sidney's thought. For Fortune is an irrational. It cannot be comprehended or intellectualized. It is the school of Patience, making Patience, indeed, the prime virtue, man's prime necessity too. Patience is different from all the virtues that inhere in Sidneian love or Aristotelian magnanimity. It leans on and demands the transcendent. It is the point at which the human discovers the divine. Sidney knew too much to distort the facts. It would have been easy to rest in a humanism of virtue as its own reward and love as its own secured delight. It would also have been cheap. One of the great moments in the book is when Musidorus and Pamela—the virtuous and successful lovers—are captured, by chance, and taken back for trial on a capital charge. Musidorus cries:

'Most excellent lady . . . in what case think you I am with myself, how unmerciful judgments do I lay upon my soul, now that I know not what god hath so reversed my well-meaning enterprise, that, instead of doing you that honour which I hoped, and not without reason hoped, Thessalia would have yielded unto you, I am now like to become a wretched instrument of your discomfort? Alas! how contrary an end have all the inclinations of my mind taken: my faith falls out a treason unto you, and the true honour I bear you is the field wherein your dishonour is like to be sown! but I invoke that universal and only wisdom, which examining the depth of hearts, hath not his judgment fixed upon the event, to bear witness with me that my desire, though in extremest vehemency, did not so overcharge my remembrance, but that as far as man's will might be extended I sought to prevent all things that might fall to your hurt.'[31]

Whatever God has reversed the well-meaning enterprise, it is neither a heathen nor a conventional renaissance Cupid. The lovers discover more than Love or even Virtue. And the discovery is made through Patience, after the storms and other hard plights they are made to endure at the hands of 'the well-wayting handmayd'.

* * *

The ground-plan of Sidney's own heroical poem is, then, the exemplification of 'patience and magnanimity'. It is not, as Milton over rashly asserted, merely 'vain and amatorious'. It is, on the contrary, as sage and serious as Spenser, or as anything Milton himself could have wished. The plan requires that the classical, romance and chivalric schemes should be brought within the orbit of an instructed renaissance Christianity. (There is no mistaking the purely Christian tone of Pamela's prayer, or of the arguments whereby Pyrocles is dissuaded from suicide.) Sidney gives an extra dimension both to the heathen virtue of Cicero and to Love as the troubadour handled it. His poem takes in ethics, politics, philosophy, handles them within the frame of the pastoral, modulates them into 'literature', and offers them to an audience that demanded both entertainment and instruction, delight and profitable pastime. The *Arcadia* in one sense is a deliberate compendium. It includes such a diversity of matters as, in Shakespeare, for example, requires three different forms: the History-play, the tragedy, and the romance itself—this last maybe Shakespeare's reaction to a renewed interest in Sidney's work.

Sidney assimilated much, but his originality consists in the massive reconciliations effected—effected coolly and comprehensively, with what Fulke Greville might call *ironia*, the power to do great things and make them appear easy, the ability to carry the heaviest loads and yet make it appear to be all a game. The pastoral-romantic-heroic-philosophical prose-poem is Sidney's great synthesis. The detail might be derivative, the idea of applying such a plan acquired at second-hand, but its originality lies in the scope and the fineness of the execution. The *Arcadia* is Sidney's Christian epic 'under the name of a romance'. As such it stands not with Montemayor, but with Tasso, Ariosto, Spenser, and (ultimately) Milton himself. Sidney, as Sir William Temple felt, is in the very first flight of European renaissance 'makers': Sir William, indeed, placed him *primus inter pares*, 'the greatest poet and noblest genius'.

Sir William's view is not the eccentricity of an aristocratic crank. It is indeed a rating that can educate us in our contemporary evaluations of the Elizabethan. When the eighteenth century looked behind itself for the sublime, the informed, the classical, and the protestantly sober it saw Milton. When the nineteenth century retrospected it saw Milton and Shakespeare. The seventeenth century could see past Milton to Sidney, and when it thought of Shakespeare it thought of him as 'natural', 'wild', or 'rude'; someone raw but also a genius, someone not exactly barbarous but at the same time not representative of the cultivated, the consciously disciplined, and the civilized. Though weighing the one against the other is like comparing the perfections of Philoclea with those of Pamela, when we place Shakespeare alongside Sidney we can see what the seventeenth century meant.

The analogy of Philoclea and Pamela is in fact an appropriate one for considering Sidney and Shakespeare together. The main difference between them lies in what might be called a *declared consciousness*. Politics, ethics, and religion (and the deliberate literary intention which controls the way these are presented)—Sidney's is a declared consciousness in each field he enters. He writes only after he has fully elucidated his purpose and his philosophy. With Shakespeare, on the other hand, we are watching all the time a process of growth: something that achieves, I think, completeness of statement and full elucidation, but which operates as much with chance as with choice; something tentative, happy, opportunistic and rapid; full of surprises, excitements and pitfalls; something, in the end, that could lead us to say that Nature takes the pen from him. Shakespeare's consciousness is not always, and not equally, declared. His ethics, psychology, religion, and literary intentions are all matters for deduction and interpretation—sometimes even for surmise. In short, it might be said, where Shakespeare expresses an Elizabethan humanity, Sidney expresses an Elizabethan education—and the disadvantages are not always with education.

Sidney and Shakespeare have, of course, a great deal in common. *King Lear*, for example, shares more with the *Arcadia* than the story which Shakespeare transformed into the sub-plot of his play. Both *King Lear* and the *Arcadia* are studies in Christian patience. They accept the same fundamental truths of the spirit and arrive at similar conclusions. Both Sidney and Shakespeare are Elizabethan and Christian, writing in a tradition that comes down to them on one side from the Middle Ages. But in everything except this basic agreement—in their modes of reaching their conclusions in their methods of presenting them—they are diametrically opposed.

The differences are bound up, I think, with the differences in their social placing. Sidney is the member of the Great House, the almost-successor to William the Silent as head of a European league against Spain. He is the friend of Languet and translator of du Plessis Mornay. The *Arcadia* is Great House literature—along with the *Faerie Queene*, the greatest work the Elizabethan Great House produces. It has the range, the lucidity and assuredness, the independence and lofty sobriety, of the Great House. Shakespeare, on the other hand, is the country grammar-school boy newly come to town. When we say this, of course, we must remember the nature of the countryside Shakespeare came from, and the nature of the town he wrote for. We must remember, too, Shakespeare's incredible capacity for growth. However, it is significant—as we suggested—that when Shakespeare first responded to the impact of the machiavellian in politics he produced Richard III, something raw and callow compared with the conception of Amphialus. Shakespeare grew, naturally. But it is only his maturest work that suggests a pattern maybe even wider than Sidney's plan. And to say this is to do injustice to neither. Sidney or Shakespeare are the two giants of the Elizabethan scene: twin miracles, like Sidney's heroines, of choice and chance, of nurture and nature. That the two are so different and yet have such profound affinities, indicates the unity in diversity of the Elizabethan scene. The scion of the Great House and the tradesman's son from the country are necessary to illuminate and explain each other.

CHAPTER THREE

Sidney and the Late-Shakespearian Romance

In *The Use of Poetry and the Use of Criticism* Mr. Eliot wrote: 'The works of Sir Philip Sidney, excepting a few sonnets, are not among those to which one can return for perpetual refreshment; the *Arcadia* is a monument of dullness.'[1]

Miss Mona Wilson, too, finds the *Arcadia* something of a trial: 'But the more we appreciate Sidney's ingenuity the more full-heartedly shall we echo Hazlitt's judgment that the result is one of the greatest monuments of the abuse of intellectual power on record.'[2]

Miss Wilson is referring particularly to Sidney's revised version of the original story. And Book II, it must be admitted, is both complex and involved. The stories proliferate, and one story will intersect another at times unnecessarily. Fresh characters are constantly making appearance, old ones reappear after we have forgotten the parts they have already played. Sidney can be over-elaborate. His involutions can both confuse and exasperate. At the same time, however, Mr. Eliot's and Miss Wilson's disparagement is rather excessive. As we have tried to show, the *Arcadia* has a grand design. The various stories introduced into Book II are not merely random concatenations of incident. They are, on the contrary, planned *exempla*, necessary parts of the map Sidney was constructing. They are articulated into the large scheme, and *belong*. They give the *Arcadia* its distinctive range, variety, and scope—the compendiousness which recommended it to Greville and the whole of the seventeenth century. Before passing to a brief view of Shakespeare's Last Period in the light of the *Arcadia* it might be advisable to glance more extensively at the matter in its compendium—particularly at the things Shakespeare and Sidney have in common and which reveal their community of thought and attitude.

Besides letting us see 'how to set a good countenance upon all the discountenances of adversitie', Greville also claimed that the *Arcadia* could provide an almost complete guide to political wisdom. Concern with the question of good government runs through the whole of the book. The two princes are themselves as it were serving an apprenticeship in the art of ruling well. 'Politic matters', Sidney was well aware, 'receive not geometrical certainties', so there is no text-book presentation of political maxims. The general picture that can be composed is one of enlightened aristocracy. Sidney has no reverence, however, for 'degree' except as it is grounded in virtue. That is the 'natural imperiousness' which 'rests in a well-formed spirit'.[3] The aristocracy will submit to a monarch—but the monarch will be limited by his own defects of virtue, and the caution he must always exercise not to unleash those powerful forces that wait all the time to break out the moment he shows himself weak or unwise. Sidney has a cool eye, and always we get the impression of a man who can look down on the machinery of government from above, whose perceptiveness is the result of first-hand acquaintance, and whose dry light is that of a mind that can not only see but see through. Here, for example, is his account of the confusion attendant on a king's death when the succession is not decided:

'Altogether like a falling steeple, the parts whereof, as windows, stones, and pinnacles were well, but the whole mass ruinous. And this was the general cause of all, wherein notwithstanding was an extreme medley of diversified thoughts, the great men looking to make themselves strong by factions, the gentlemen some bending to them, some standing upon themselves, some desirous to overthrow those few which they thought were over them; the soldiers desirous of trouble, as the nurse of spoil, and not much unlike to them though in another way, were all the needy sort, the rich fearful, the wise careful. This composition of conceits brought forth a dangerous tumult, which yet would have been more dangerous, but that it had so many parts that nobody well knew against whom chiefly to oppose themselves.'[4]

This is typically Sidneian. First we get the brilliant visual image so well capable of carrying a moral—the steeple falling, still maintaining the appearance of cohesion, none of the parts broken 'but the whole mass ruinous'; then the translation of the image into terms of confusion in the commonweal, great men, gentry, soldiery, and 'all the needy sort'; finally, the use of his favourite dialectic in the last sentence (an abstract statement of what the image of the falling steeple implied) showing how absolute lack of cohesion has itself a kind of safety in it or can at least indefinitely postpone disaster—the steeple now falling for an indefinitely long time, a perfect form in the air that the least touch will dissipate utterly.

Pyrocles and Musidorus will ultimately be ideal governors like Euarchus. They are plentifully supplied in the *Arcadia* with knowledge of bad rulers. Sidney varies his examples, but the variations are all on the theme of a wrenching away from the frame of nature. Plexirtus, for example (he is Shakespeare's Edmund), ousted his brother Leonatus (Shakespeare's Edgar) by machiavellian practice. The parallel story of Plangus and his step-mother gives almost a recipe for perversion of a king's mind so that the truth will seem to him a lie, and the rightful heir be forced to flee the country. The queen in this instance makes use of a tool-villain:

'Then took she help to her of a servant near about her husband, whom she knew to be of a hasty ambition, and such a one, who, wanting true sufficiency to raise him, would make a ladder of any mischief. Him she useth to deal more plainly in alleging causes of jealousy, making him know the fittest times when her husband already was stirred that way. And so they two, with divers ways, nourished one humour, like musicians, that singing divers parts, make one music. He sometimes with fearful countenance would desire the king to look to himself, for that all the court and city were full of whisperings and expectations of some sudden change, upon what ground himself knew not. Another time he would counsel the king to make much of his son, and hold his favour, for that it was too late now to keep him under. Now seeming to fear himself, because, he said, Plangus loved none of them that were great about his father. Lastly, breaking with him directly, making a sorrowful countenance, and an humble gesture bear false witness for his true meaning, that he found not only soldiery but people weary of his government, and all their affection bent upon Plangus; both he and the queen concurring in strange dreams, and each thing else, that in a mind already perplexed might breed astonishment: so that within a while, all Plangus's actions began to be translated into the language of suspicion. Which though Plangus found, yet could he not avoid, even contraries being driven to draw one yoke of argument. If he were magnificent, he spent much with an aspiring intent, if he spared, he heaped much with an aspiring intent; if he spoke courteously, he angled the people's hearts; if he were silent, he mused upon some dangerous plot. In sum, if he could have turned himself to as many forms as Proteus every form should have been made hideous . . . the more he protested, the more his father thought he dissembled, accounting his integrity to be but a cunning face of falsehood.'[5]

Counterpointing this story of the uxorious king and his base-born wife there is the story of Erona and Antiphilus—the over-fond queen who married beneath her. Antiphilus had been helped originally by Pyrocles and Musidorus. When 'the two paragons of virtue' leave him his nature is unable to withstand the temptations of absolute power:

'Antiphilus I say, being crowned and delivered from the presence of those two, whose virtues, while they were present, like good schoolmasters, suppressed his vanities, he had not strength of mind enough in him to make long delay of discovering what manner of man he was. But straight like one carried up to so high a place that he loseth the discerning of the ground over which he is, so was his mind lifted so far beyond the level of his own discourse, that remembering only that himself was in the high seat of a king, he could not perceive that he was a king of reasonable creatures who would quickly scorn follies and repine at injuries. But imagining no so true property of sovereignty as to do what he listed, and to list whatsoever pleased his fancy, he quickly made his kingdom a tennis-court, where his subjects should be the balls, not in truth cruelly, but licentiously abusing them, presuming so far upon himself, that what he did was liked of everybody: nay, that his disgraces were favours, and all because he was a king. For in nature not able to perceive the bounds of great matters, suddenly borne into an unknown ocean of absolute power, he was swayed withal, he knew not how, as every wind of passion puffed him.'[6]

The stories of Erona and Antiphilus, and of Andromana and Plangus are only two of the episodes of Book II. Their adjectival force and relevance are apparent. Adjusted to the main theme, they suggest the dark side of Arcadia—the evil that the lovers must overcome in the world and in themselves in order that their mutual perfections might be maintained. The lapse from virtue, the surrender of the will to passion, sets up an inward tempest that soon brings about external disorder, and 'an evil mind in authority doth not only follow the sway of the desires already within it, but frames to itself new desires not before thought of'.[7] A striking thing about the Sidneian universe is its similarity to Shakespeare's in structure. The technique whereby Plangus is blackened to his father is familiar to us in Iago and Edmund. Shakespeare's villains too are either the slaves of passion or the resolved rejectors of the frame of Nature. Defection in the private world leads, for both, to dissolution of the public amities and concord. And the strategy of flight—the only possible one in such circumstances as Plangus finds himself surrounded by—is the strategy Edgar adopts, and Pericles, Polixenes, and Camillo after him. Sidney and the later Shakespeare would both agree on the moral mechanisms at work. They are embraced by the same community of ideas.

The Sidneian heroical poem is, then, compendious. Its material is deliberately moralized. Nothing is included which does not exhibit the intellectual scheme Sidney has in mind—a scheme which must treat of Virtue in relation to politics; Virtue in 'the school of affection' where desire will be taken up into an ideal wholeness of mind maintained by two; Virtue, finally, set in the wider frame of adversity, confronted by the irrationals of chance as well as by the irrationals of wrong choice, Virtue tried by Fortune until it arrives at the transcendent patience and is transformed into a reason above reason: for Virtue is not enough:

> *man's virtue is but part of man,*
> *And part must follow where whole man doth go.*[8]

We have already quoted Milton's adverse comment on the Sidneian world. Another and more equable Miltonic statement is also appropriate. In *Paradise Lost*, Book IX, Milton deplores the degenerate notions of heroical poetry, and holds up against these his loftier conception:

> *Warrs, hitherto the onely Argument*
> *Heroic deem'd, chief maistrie to dissect*
> *With long and tedious havoc fabled Knights*
> *In Battels feign'd; the better fortitude*
> *Of Patience and Heroic martyrdom*
> *Unsung.*[9]

Sidney would undoubtedly agree. Milton is almost echoing the 'patience and magnanimitie' of the *Apologie*. Sidney's own poem covers the better as well as the worse fortitude. Its most characteristic moments are such climaxes as when captive good must maintain its ground against captive ill: as when the three prisoners are brought out and threatened with beheading:

'A sight full of pity it was, to see these three (all excelling in all those excellencies wherewith nature can beautify anybody: Pamela giving sweetness to majesty; Philoclea enriching nobleness with humbleness, Zelmane setting in womanly beauty manlike valour) to be thus subjected to the basest injury of unjust fortune. One might see in Pamela a willingness to die, rather than to have life at other's discretion; though sometimes a princely disdain would sparkle out of her princely eyes, that it should be in other's power to force her to die. In Philoclea a pretty fear came up, to endamask her rosy cheeks: but it was such a fear, as rather seemed a kindly child to her innate humbleness, than any other dismayedness; or if she was dismayed it was more for Zelmane, than for herself; or if more for herself, it was because Zelmane should lose her.'[10]

This is a nice example of Sidney's art. The verbal pattern never remains a matter of merely verbal play. The external formalism reflects a vital inner unity of thought. Virtue in the romance world is the apex of a pyramid, or the point of intersection of two worlds. It is comprehensive, a consummation. So one way of expressing it is by accumulation amounting to hyperbole, 'giving sweetness to majesty . . . enriching nobleness with humbleness . . . setting in womanly beauty manlike valour'—the reconciliation of opposites that erected wit can achieve and express. But another way is just as possible: a *via negativa*, such as the fine series of discriminations that suggest so exactly Pamela's willingness to die that is not a wish to be rid of life, or Philoclea's fear and dismay that are neither timidity nor depression. The spiritual experience, the intellectual lucidity, and the literary gift displayed in passages such as this remind us of those similar ones responsible for Cordelia, Samson, or St. Thomas refuting the Fourth Tempter.

If the manner of Sidney's style is finely adapted to his matter, the form of the heroical romance on a large scale, as we have maintained, also images the world-view Sidney holds. Conversely, to hand on the form of the romance to any successor was to hand on something of the philosophy implied. Orientated towards perfection—which must be presented as fully incarnate in the achieved relation between two lovers, a prince and a princess—the romance world then has four spheres that are interlocked. There is first the sphere of virtue and attained perfection; then the sphere of human imperfection, political and passionate, surrounding and likely at any minute to threaten the first; around these again, the sphere of non-human accident, chance, or misfortune, the sphere of the sea and storms; and finally, enclosing all, the sphere of the transcendent, guaranteeing after the 'storm or other hard plights' that the ending will be a happy one—granted patience.

The form could take in as much or as little of the fully elaborated philosophy as its users were capable of supplying. At the popular extreme (as, for example, in Greene's *Pandosto*) there would merely be a Renaissance novellette, with hardships, pathos, Greek names, and a wishful prosperity in the conclusion. Or the form might lend itself to something dignified, consolatory, and Boethian (as the first two acts of *Pericles* seem to be). Boethius was indeed a main source for rationalizations of chance and mischance. Translated by Chaucer and by Queen Elizabeth, a Jacobean version appeared in 1609. Throughout the medieval period Boethius was regarded as a Christian. His thought on Fortune in any case readily adapts itself to a Christian mode of thinking:

'Thou hast now knowen and attaint the doutous or double visage of thilke blinde goddesse Fortune . . . she, that is now cause of so muche sorwe to thee, sholde been cause to thee of pees and of joye. . . . Thus, at the laste, it behoveth thee to suffren with evene wille in pacience al that is don in-with the floor of Fortune.'[11]

Boethius uses the imagery of the sea of Fortune, and of storm and thunder, to express the irrationals of the third sphere. Like Perdita, he knows that

affliction may subdue the cheek
But not take in the mind
(*Winter's Tale*, IV. iv. 589–90)

and, like Prospero, that Fortune is, to the right-wise, 'now my good Lady':

'thanne is alle fortune good, the which fortune is certein that it be either rightful or elles profitable'.[12]

But Boethius occupies an ambiguous no-man's land between benevolent Deism and Christianity. In him there is certainly the attempt to marry the rational and the irrational in a supreme transcendent. But in him, too, there is the danger of negation, of cancelling out both good fortune and bad, reducing both to the same thing, leaving the virtuous man with nothing finally except a vacuous impassiveness. Milton was aware of the crucial difference between the patience that is truly Christian and that which is merely classical. His fallen angels in the great adversity of Hell he made into Stoics, as they sat

> *on a Hill retir'd*
> *In thoughts more elevate, and reason'd high*
> *Of Providence, Foreknowledge, Will, and Fate,*
> *Fixt Fate, free will, foreknowledge absolute,*
> *And found no end, in wandring mazes lost.*
> *Of good and evil much they argued there,*
> *Of happiness and final misery,*
> *Passion and Apathie, and glory, and shame,*
> *Vain wisdom all, and false Philosophie:*
> *Yet with a pleasing sorcerie could charm*
> *Pain for a while, and anguish, and excite*
> *Fallacious hope, or arm th'obdured brest*
> *With stubborn patience as with triple steel.*[13]

But Christian patience is a different thing from the Stoic. Neither stubborn nor impassive (Pamela and Philoclea express it) it finds its greatest expression in Christus Patiens. It is a release of charity. It suffers long because it is kind, and its kindness remains. It loves its enemies who slay it. It marries the two worlds, forgives, and redeems as it unites. Milton brings to the heroical poem his fullest realization of 'Patience and Heroic martyrdom'. In Sidney too the form can take the full stress and play of all those insights compounded in his transcendental renaissance humanism. In Beaumont and Fletcher, on the other hand, the romance supplies a happy ending to an evil that in itself is irredeemable and inconsolable—so that the happiness of Beaumont's dénouements is like the rictus on a corpse, his romances like the falling steeple Sidney knew, 'the parts whereof, as windows, stones, and pinnacles were well, but the whole mass ruinous'. Or, in Shakespeare, more explicitly Christian in his terms than Sidney, but within the same tradition of heroical Christian humanism, the romance could serve to round off the experience of the tragic period—and at the same time join hands with the popular novellette of Greene, supplying entertainment and relaxation, the conclusion of a project 'which was to please'. Shakespeare's final period we might now look at in the light of the Arcadian world that preceded it and which Shakespeare knew.

* * *

Shakespeare's Last Period begins with a storm and ends with *The Tempest.* Storms may be archetypal. They were certainly traditional for all those who knew the *De Consolatione*. For those who did not, but had read Sidney, there was always the ancestral shipwreck of Pyrocles and Musidorus. Part of this we have already quoted. (Its 'ship, or rather the carcase of a ship' might reappear in Prospero's 'rotten carcase of a butt'.) The other part —separated from the first by more than a whole book—is equally worth examination. Intrinsically interesting, it is also important as a pointer to the meaning as well as the provenance of the 'symbols' Shakespeare incorporates into his last plays:

'But by that the next morning began a little to make a gilded show of a good meaning, there arose even with the sun, a veil of dark clouds before his face, which, shortly, like ink poured into water, had blacked over all the face of the heaven, preparing as it were a mournful stage for a tragedy to be played on. For forthwith the winds began to speak louder, and, as in a tumultuous kingdom, to think themselves fittest instruments of commandments; and blowing whole storms of hail and rain upon them, they were sooner in danger, than they could almost bethink themselves of change. For then the traitorous sea began to swell in pride against the afflicted navy, under which, while the heaven favoured them, it had lain so calmly, making mountains of itself, over which the tossed and tottering ship should climb, to be straight carried down again to a pit of hellish darkness; with such cruel blows against the sides of the ship that, which way soever it went, was still in his malice, that there was left neither power to stay nor way to escape. And shortly had it so dissevered the loving company, which the day before had tarried together, that most of them never met again, but were swallowed up in his never satisfied mouth. Some indeed, as since was shown, after long wandering, returned into Thessalia, others recovered Byzantium, and served Euarchus in his war. But the ship wherein the princes were, now left as much alone as proud lords be when fortune fails them, though they employed all industry to save themselves, yet what they did was rather for duty to nature than hope to escape, so ugly darkness, as if it would prevent the night's coming, usurped the day's right: which accompanied sometimes with thunders, always with horrible noises of the chafing winds, made the masters and pilots so astonished that they knew not how to direct, and if they knew, they could scarcely, when they directed, hear their own whistle. For the sea strove with the winds which should be louder, and the shrouds of the ship, with a gastful noise to them that were in it, witnessed that their ruin was the wager of the others' contention, and the heaven roaring out thunders the more amazed them, as having those powers for enemies. Certainly there is no danger carries with it more horror than that which grows in those floating kingdoms. For that dwelling place is unnatural to mankind, and then the terribleness of the continual motion, the desolation of the far-being from comfort, the eye and the ear having ugly images ever before it, doth still vex the mind, even when it is best armed against it. But thus the day passed, if that might be called day, while the cunningest mariners were so conquered by the storm that they thought it best with stricken sails to yield to be governed by it: the valiantest feeling inward dismayedness, and yet the fearfullest ashamed fully to show it, seeing that the princes, who were to part from the greatest fortunes, did in their countenances accuse no point of fear, but encouraging them to do what might be done, putting their hands to every most painful office, taught them in one instant to promise themselves the best, and yet to despise the worst. But so were they carried by the tyranny of the wind, and the treason of the sea all that night, which the older it was, the more wayward it showed itself towards them: till the next morning, known to be a morning better by the hour-glass than by the day's clearness, having run fortune so blindly, as itself ever was painted, lest the conclusion should not answer to the rest of the play, they were driven upon a rock, which, hidden with those outrageous waves, did, as it were, closely dissemble his cruel mind, till with an unbelieved violence, but them to that have tried it, the ship ran upon it, and seeming willinger to perish than to have her course stayed, redoubled her blows, till she had broken herself in pieces, and as it were, tearing out her own bowels to feed the seas greediness, left nothing within it but despair of safety and expectation of a loathsome end. There was to be seen the divers manners of minds in distress: some sat upon the top of the poop weeping and wailing, till the sea swallowed them; some one more able to abide death than the fear of death, cut his own throat to prevent drowning; some prayed: and there wanted not of them which cursed, as if the heavens could not be more angry than they were. . . . But the princes, using the passions of fearing evil, and desiring to escape only to serve the rule of virtue, not to abandon one's self, leaped to a rib of the ship, which broken from his fellows, floated with more likelihood to do service than any other limb of that ruinous body.'[14]

Sidney's romance is important because it has such inner coherence—a large, mature, and conscious philosophy. We are protected, with him, from projecting on to him meanings of our own, or finding in him answers to needs of ours he himself did not share and did not intend to answer. In his storm we can confidently follow his own moralizations.

The opening of the passage is conventional enough: morning set out with 'a gilded show of a good meaning' then rapidly changed: appearances are deceitful, and fortune fickle. The sun was veiled, the heavens darkened. Then comes the deliberate suggestion of stage-management in the scene—'as it were a mournful stage for a tragedy to be played on'—which works in two ways. Nature behaves in such a theatrical way because nature in fact does have to follow a 'plot': all the happenings in nature are meaningful, obedient to a design which may not be fully apparent. Secondly, by pointing to this element of deliberate manipulation in nature Sidney removes from his highly mannered description of the storm—'artificial' as it seems—any suggestion of insincerity. The patterned prose that imitates nature imitates her not by external realism but by bringing out the inner design in accordance with which she operates. The spectator of the tragedy is *nearer* to the full reality than the actor in the tragedy itself. The references to the theatre are continued in the next sentence: 'forthwith the winds began to speak louder' like actors in Cambysses' vein, and then quickly the imagery slips into that of the tumultuous kingdoms Elizabethan tragedy celebrates, and the winds become usurping and contentious rebels. The idea of revolt and treachery continues and along with this goes 'pride', the root of all such evil ever since the first revolt. It is only at this point that Sidney then brings in the visualized sea 'making mountains of itself, over which the tossed and tottering ship should climb, to be straight carried down again to the pit of hellish darkness'. The word 'hellish' takes on a livelier meaning for the saturation of the passage in moral suggestion which has preceded it. The personification of the sea we do not object to: the sea, we have already accepted, is itself an agent, the meaning of the total drama in which it plays its part is also a human one—something that the human beings who are at the centre of the storm will only understand in the course of an experience of tempest which fully reveals to them their own nature and that of the designer of the play. Further, the sea can do no more and no worse in the way of destruction than human beings themselves can do. The third sphere of chance misfortunes is not much different in effect from the second sphere of human malice. The sea, in fact, is almost equated with the tyrant or rebel. The princes are cut off from their friends and left in their ship as in a prison, 'as much alone as proud lords be when fortune fails them'. Like Pericles, however,

> *galling*
> *His kingly hands with hauling of the ropes*
> (IV. i. 53–4)

or knowing, like Ferdinand, that

> *some kinds of baseness*
> *Are nobly undergone* (*The Tempest*, III. i. 2–3)

Pyrocles and Musidorus set an example to their crew by 'putting their hands to every most painful office'. But the ship is doomed nevertheless. The tyranny of the wind and the treachery of a rock (the enemy under cover is a permanent agent of disaster for the Elizabethans) finally bring the inevitable upon them. Sidney's concluding sentences are important. A storm reveals the innermost nature of those exposed to it, 'the divers manners of minds in distress'. The princes themselves have been exemplary in their conduct. They act 'from duty to nature rather than hope to escape so ugly a darkness', 'using the passions of fearing evil, and desiring to escape only to serve the rule of virtue'. The rest behave much like those in the first scene of *The Tempest*: some commit suicide, some pray, some curse God. Thus the first and the fourth spheres too are brought into the passage—virtue that will not admit defeat from fortune, and will not submit because of its implicit patience, its confidence that defeat and victory can be married because of the transcendent. By the time the storm has been fully described we are made aware of all the main parts of the Sidneian universe.

Pericles, Shakespeare's first 'romance', clearly follows the established pattern. Gower, summing up at the end of the play, gives a more adequate account of what has taken place than most Epilogues are accustomed to do:

In Antiochus and his daughter you have heard
Of monstrous lust the due and just reward:
In Pericles, his queen, and daughter, seen—
Although assail'd with fortune fierce and keen—
Virtue preserved from fell destruction's blast,
Led on by heaven, and crown'd with joy at last.
In Helicanus you may well descry
A figure of truth, of faith, of loyalty.
In reverend Cerimon there still appears
The worth that learned charity aye wears.
For wicked Cleon and his wife, when fame
Had spread their cursed deed, and honour'd name
Of Pericles, to rage the city turn,
That him and his they in his palace burn:
The gods for murder seemed so content
To punish them; although not done, but meant.
So on your patience evermore attending,
New joy wait on you! Here our play hath ending.

The play begins with the prince risking his life for the hand of the princess. She seems outwardly ideal:

apparell'd like the spring,
Graces her subjects, and her thoughts the king
Of every virtue gives renown to men. (I. i. 12–14)

But this 'glorious casket' is 'stor'd with ill'. She is living incestuously with her father, and Pericles reads the riddle. His speech records the mystique of virginity and the shock of the fall from the ideal:

You're a fair viol, and your sense the strings,
Who, finger'd to make man his lawful music,
Would draw heaven down and all the gods to hearken;
But being play'd upon before your time,
Hell only danceth at so harsh a chime. (I. i. 81–5)

Pericles is naturally revolted, and he knows he is in possession of a dangerous secret. Antiochus, having broken one law, will not stop short of breaking any others. In him law is merely the tyrant's will. Antiochus knows he has been discovered, but like Cecropia in the *Arcadia* he will wear the vizor of virtue. Pericles, however, is aware of his danger:

How courtesy would seem to cover sin,
When what is done is like an hypocrite,
The which is good in nothing but in sight. (I. i. 121–3)

He determines to save himself by running away:

Then, lest my life be cropp'd to keep you clear
By flight I'll shun the danger which I fear. (I. i. 125–6)

Antiochus—again, like Sidney's Plexirtus—procures a convenient villain-courtier to pursue Pericles and kill him.

Back in his own kingdom, Pericles is still afraid of Antiochus's vengeance: the more so that his subjects as well as himself will be drawn into the suffering. He determines on further flight. He calls for Helicanus, the good servant and no flatterer, and hands over the kingdom to him, 'the figure of truth, of faith, and loyalty'. Unlike Antiochus, Pericles recognizes that both princes and subjects are submitted to virtue, and that kings in this are servants to those they rule. Helicanus is

> *Fit counsellor and servant for a prince,*
> *Who by thy wisdom mak'st a prince thy servant.*
> (I. ii. 63–4)

This is the ethic of the Arcadian world. Helicanus, too, voices an Arcadian wisdom. He tells Pericles

> *To bear with patience*
> *Such griefs as you do lay upon yourself,* (I. ii. 65–6)

just as, later, Leontes will be urged to do as the heavens have done:

> *forget your evil;*
> *With them forgive yourself*—(*Winter's Tale*, v. i. 5–6)

And just as the Boatswain knows in *The Tempest* that there is a proper self-love as an improper. So Pericles is in flight once more. We next see him landing in famine-stricken Tharsus, relieving the distress of Cleon and Dionyza, a king and queen in adversity. Pericles' troubles continue. Having left Tharsus, he is once more on the sea, and soon shipwrecked. The second act opens with him walking up on the beach, a sole survivor. In adversity he is studiously correct, resigned rather than rebellious:

> *Yet cease your ire, you angry stars of heaven!*
> *Wind, rain, and thunder, remember earthly man*
> *Is but a substance that must yield to you:*
> *And I, as fits my nature, to obey you.*
> *Alas, the sea hath cast me on the rocks,*
> *Wash'd me from shore to shore, and left me breath*
> *Nothing to think on but ensuing death:*
> *Let it suffice the greatness of your powers*
> *To have bereft a prince of all his fortunes:*
> *And having thrown him from yon watery grave*
> *Here to have death in peace is all I crave.* (II. i. 1–11)

Pericles meets the two fishermen who read the moral of the sea —that it is very like the land, for there too big fish eat the little ones—and his armour is restored to him, dredged up in the fishermen's nets. Pericles is now enabled to go to the king's court and take part in the tourney for the hand of the king's daughter. Simonides is a good ruler, one of those who are

A model which heaven makes like to itself. (II. ii. 11)

Subordinate princes

sit, like stars, about his throne,
And he the sun for them to reverence. (II. iii. 39–40)

He has the king-like reason, too, which remembers the difference between outward show and inward reality:

Opinion's but a fool, that makes us scan
The outward habit by the inward man. (II. ii. 56–7)

Pericles wins the tournament and the princess's love. Thaisa in fact will have Pericles whether her father will or no (a recurrent *motif* in the romances). Simonides pretends to wrath that she is so wilful and stages an apparent choice for her between love and filial obedience. The anger is, however, only a loving game and all ends happily.

Up to this point we have been following the first two acts of *Pericles*—work only doubtfully Shakespeare's, and almost certainly not of Shakespeare's later period. It is surprising how much of the substance of the late Shakespearian romance these acts contain or adumbrate: how, certainly, they seem to incorporate in coda-form features that could be strictly paralleled in the *Arcadia*. The mystique of virginity; the beautiful appearance and the corrupt heart; the tyrant thrown from the frame of nature and reason by 'blood' or appetite; the tyrant wearing the vizor of kindness, employing a court-henchman to commit his murders; the contrast of the good governor; and of the unfortunate ruler who has, fortunately, a good servant whom he can make vicegerent; the strategy of flight before the 'tempest' of passionate malice; the sea; resignation after shipwreck; the winning of a princess in the end, after the storm and other hard plights; the virgin-boldness of the love which is more absolute and inward than obedience to a father's will; the hinted opposition between the two, and the evasion of any real conflict on this issue—chapter and verse could be given for almost every detail.

If we suppress comparison of these first two acts with the three that follow, we must admit that in their own way they are surprisingly good: good enough, as Shakespeare himself must have considered, to stand as prologue to what he himself would add. What prevents us from admitting they are fully Shakespearian?

First, whatever effectiveness or coherence they have is derivative. They are parasitic on a system which stands behind them. From this system parts are abstracted and then reassembled. Reports themselves, the such a summary outline as we have made suggests there is more in the original than in fact is there. For the first two acts suggest more than they can sustain. Secondly, the absence might be noted of any inclusive consciousness in the first two acts—a consciousness centred either in a single character, made capable of investing all the parts with significance, or a consciousness centred in the writer of the acts and made pervasively present through the verse or the general moral sensitivity. The first two acts abound in moral precepts which are made to substitute for moral occasions. There is no one capable of embracing the whole, no one who serves to bring together all the parts of the moral universe implied, as Pamela does in the *Arcadia*. There is no one, in fact, who seems as securely centred as are any of the four lovers in the *Arcadia*, or as even Cecropia in her perversity, and Amphialus in his error. Pericles himself is driven by a *vis a tergo*. The mechanics of the moral world are too obvious and too obviously automatic. There is no suggestion here, as there is all the time in the *Arcadia*, of the operative tensions within the sphere of Fortune and Adversity. The copyist of the Sidneian world (assuming that it is with such we have to deal) is insensitive to those things in the Sidneian universe which make it more than a daydream: the pressure of resolution or patience that is resistant to Fortune, the pressure of passion that combines with her irrationals generally, the room for growth and for disastrous collapse that Sidney always retains. The version of the Sidneian world presented in the first two acts is comparatively crude. The whole scheme is rendered inert. At the key points of the action where in Sidney we should expect convincing statements of virtue and patience as apices of the mind—and expect them to be given in those analyses and differentiations Sidney's prose is so capable of—we get instead something surprisingly flat. A good example is Pericles' resignation after his shipwreck. Each of the parts—in this instance the 'angry stars', the imagery of 'wind, rain, and thunder', the sea that has washed him 'from shore to shore', etc.—seems to recall a prior Shakespearian occasion. But actually, the moral and verbal sensitivity is simply lacking. We are left with the lowest common factors in each case: verbal formulae instead of poetic statement, the cliché of resignation instead of the vast moment of spiritual forces that turns on 'patience'. In the hands of the writer of the first two acts the romance-world degenerates into one in which nothing can really happen. We are given no sense of the creaturely, of the existential, of being at the centre of organic change. We are left, that is, with no sense of people as people. The use of the traditional scheme can rise only as high as the reporting of moral precepts, and the presentation of what Milton would call 'Apathie' rather than that activation which compels fresh choice and new endeavour.

The late-Shakespearian appears decisively with the first words Pericles utters on his appearance in Act III, Scene i. It is a short scene, but long enough to contain a storm, the announcement of a birth, the death of a wife, her committal to the sea, and three great lyrical speeches by Pericles himself—three purple patches unusual in weight and number even for Shakespeare in so short a space. The technique is typical of the late Shakespeare, however, and worth observing.

The first thing to note is, I think, the way in which the late Shakespeare can suddenly impose voices upon the stage and upon the audience. 'Suddenly', 'impose', and 'voices'—each of the words is necessary to record the new impression the late-Shakespeare makes. To use his own phrase, Shakespeare can at any moment now *take* us with beauty. If the assault were by something cruder, or if it were less finely managed, it would amount to the employment of shock-tactics:

PER. *O! how Lychorida,*
How does my queen? Thou stormest venomously;
Wilt thou spit all thyself? The seaman's whistle
Is as a whisper in the ears of death,
Unheard. Lychorida! Lucina, O!
Divinest patroness, and midwife gentle
To those that cry by night, convey thy deity
Aboard our dancing boat; make swift the pangs
Of my queen's travails!

(Enter Lychorida, with an Infant.)

Now, Lychorida!

LYCH. *Here is a thing too young for such a place,*
Who, if it had conceit, would die, as I
Am like to do: take in your arms this piece
Of your dead queen.
PER. *How, how, Lychorida!*
LYCH. *Patience, good sir, do not assist the storm.*
Here's all that is left living of your queen,
A little daughter: for the sake of it,
Be manly, and take comfort.
PER. *O you gods!*
Why do you make us love your goodly gifts
And snatch them straight away? We here below
Recall not what we give, and therein may
Use honour with you.
LYCH. *Patience, good sir,*
Even for this charge. (III. i. 6–27)

A situation highly charged with feeling is abruptly presented (we are, for example, put *in the middle* of the storm) and then we are given a close-up of the character, speaking when feeling is climactically intense. There is swiftness of transition from one tone to another: Pericles is anxious, apprehensive, and angry within the space of two lines. Then the swimming suggestion of the 'seaman's whistle . . . as a whisper in the ears of death, unheard' is floated in, with its hushing awe, its arrest of passion and tumult, its stillness in the midst of storm that almost surprises one into contemplation; and this followed immediately by the loud shout of the nurse, and this by the plea, compassionate and self-compassionate, to Lucina. The swimming suggestiveness of phrase is still in evidence—a manner which brings Shakespeare nearer to the romantics of the nineteenth century than to his contemporaries in the seventeenth. The phrase 'those that cry by night' seems to mean more than merely women in labour. Its resonance covers also all those that cry for them, and those they are bringing into the world, whose first sound is a cry. . . . Or does it? For Shakespeare's late verse is now, comparatively, a friable thing. Its aura of suggestion is shadowier than can be tabulated in terms of pun, or ambiguity, or multiple meaning. It is really an expansion of meaning beyond that which is immediately relevant or required, a constant quickening of the listener to have feelings immediately available, and a constant sudden overdraft on these. Shakespeare's late verse is a poetry of feeling. For all its richness it is simpler than the verse of the middle period:

A terrible child-bed hast thou had, my dear;
No light, no fire; the unfriendly elements
Forgot thee utterly; nor have I time
To give thee hallow'd to thy grave, but straight
Must cast thee, scarcely coffin'd, to the ooze,
Where, for a monument upon thy bones,
And aye-remaining lamps, the belching whale
And humming water must o'erwhelm thy corpse,
Lying with simple shells. (III. i. 57–65)

Dr. Tillyard has referred to 'that simple, yet strained, remote and magical note that sounds from time to time in the last plays'.[15] The note is sounded, though, very often, together with others—others that are strained and violent, strained in the suddenness of their contrasts. 'Lying with simple shells' gives one note: the adjective dissolving disdain in nostalgic envy. 'Belching whale' gives another—the monstrous, indifferent, and bestial life, and yet the mindless, contented coarseness of the creature. 'Humming water' gives yet another—the dizzying depths through which we sink to the 'simple shells', the loss of consciousness, the sound of the distant storm confused to a blind murmur, then the water itself humming as it spins in its vortices, humming like a top, still yet swirling: and as one consciousness is lost we adopt the consciousness of the sea, and death is a sleep and the sound of humming as restful as a lullaby, until we are 'lying with simple shells' in the absolute 'Apathie' we both long for and disdain.

But in addition to notes like this there is also that of a baroque self-consciousness, the manner daring of 'aye-remaining lamps'. This intrudes, too, between the intimate immediacy and naturalism of the opening lines and the imaginative moment of the closing ones. Something of self-consciousness has to be counted in to complete the description of the late-Shakespearian style: a distance to which Shakespeare projects his creation, a lack of emotional *engagement*, and yet a rich appreciation—an almost indulgent exaggeration—of the opportunity for stance any moment can bring along.

Passages such as this tempt us further than Shakespeare himself seems inclined to go. The immensely suggestive moments can lead out beyond the frame of character and beyond the frame of the theme: into the realm of 'humming water' and 'belching whale'. But Shakespeare had a frame to support him and to keep the moments coherently together. In the case of the last three acts of *Pericles* the frame is supplied by the romance world which had also served the writer of the first two acts.

For *Pericles* is a study of the prince in misfortune. The first two acts show a good man embroiled, swept from security by the tempest of another's wickedness. The misfortunes are external, the loss is the loss of a throne. The second part begins with the more inward loss of a wife, a loss however which brings the gain of a daughter, for Fortune always has a 'doutous or double visage'. Shakespeare is supported by what he has himself learnt about the inner structure of this world as well as guided by what he knows of it from others who have also explored it.

Act III begins with the tempest and ends with Pericles making provision for his daughter, the 'fresh-new seafarer', and bidding 'a priestly farewell' to his wife. Scene i is a lyrical Shakespearian handling of the matter of Patience. In his opening speech Pericles addresses the 'god of this great vast'—a deity higher than Fortune. In the first shock of his grief at hearing of Thaisa's death he is in danger of being overthrown. 'Patience, good sir,' the nurse calls to him, 'do not assist the storm,'—

Be manly and take comfort. (III. i. 22)

The force of Lychorida's last words is apt to be lost on a post-renaissance audience. 'Manly' implies the summoning-up of the full fortitude manhood implies, but also assumes in this context the creaturely dependence of that manhood: virtue cannot be self-sufficient however far it exerts itself, and even though it is asserted to the full. Pericles calls out against the gods, but it is a human bewilderment rather than a passionate revolt. Again Lychorida cries, 'Patience, good sir.' Pericles recovers himself and turns to the child. The overflow of compassion is a good augury. Only those can take comfort who can give comfort, and there is immense tenderness in Pericles' words. By the time he is finished he has found a new balance. His reply to the sailor indicates the firm hold he now has on his re-established manliness:

FIRST SAILOR. *What courage, sir? God save you!*
PER. *Courage enough. I do not fear the flaw:*
It hath done to me the worst. (III. i. 38–40)

When the sailors tell him his wife must be cast overboard he submits to the necessity. In the great speech we have already analysed he fully realizes death's final 'apathie'—away from the storm, on the sea's floor, 'lying with simple shells': an apathy which is the opposite of patience as death is the opposite of life. He bids Thaisa 'a priestly farewell'.

The difference between the first and the second parts of *Pericles* can now be more clearly seen. Instead of reporting moral precepts Shakespeare is presenting moral occasions. The audience not only has a map to the territory it can also see the movements of the protagonist across the countryside. In taking over or resuming the play Shakespeare judged rightly that what it needed was a 'voice'—the impression of a living personality, and that personality a centre of sensitive moral consciousness. The unit of communication now is the whole scene. Inside that scene we can see the complete turn or rotation of a person responding to a completely given moral occasion. Lyrically evocative as the scene is, the lyrical imagery would not be sufficient, however, without the clearly mapped territory behind it—which Shakespeare shared both with his audience and his collaborator. 'Belching whale' and 'humming water', overpoweringly suggestive as they are, are not as illuminatingly definitive as the interchange between the sailor and the bereaved husband. 'Imagery' is a deceptive word to use in connection with occasions such as this. Imagery includes more than metaphor, more even than is usually included in the phrase 'verbal texture'. Shakespeare's main controlling image is the image of a man in certain circumstances speaking from the midst of his situation to another man (Shakespeare, again, gives the Sailor a 'voice'). The flow of meaning that then takes place only has significance within the moral situation that has been presented. The emotive aura of the separable 'images' (what Aristotle called 'diction') is large and maybe vague. The total moral reference of the scene, however, is specific and precise. And the references in this case fall within the field covered by 'patience in adversity'.

The two explaining systems which have been applied recently to the interpretation of the Last Plays miss, I think, the essentially Elizabethan—and for that matter the more deeply human—inwardness of the romance scheme. The first of these has been based on the *Golden Bough* and the fertility cycle and rebirth. The second has been similarly based on the Christian conception of regeneration and resurrection. Neither, I think, is as satisfactory as the contemporary and conventional scheme which Shakespeare used. Anthropology does not take us far enough. By its insidious precipitations it tends to silt over the clear and sharp contours of the renaissance moral world. The second explaining system errs in the opposite direction. It carries us too far and too fast. It particularizes in a field of meaning beyond Shakespeare's intention—though Shakespeare, I have no doubt, would know St. Paul and the burial service, and accepted the New Testament. To theologize the last plays, however, is to distort them. Though patience as Shakespeare conceives it implies St. Paul and the New Testament, patience as Shakespeare realizes it in the Last Plays is a familiar and well-walked parish in a wider diocese. Nor is the parish presided over by the Fisher King, and in it St. Paul is taken for granted but not allegorized in every Whitsun pastoral. And this brings us to a further distortion which over-anxiety about the greatness of Shakespeare's final plays is sometimes responsible for—a distortion of their tone. Shakespeare's last plays are not conceived at the same level of seriousness as Dante's *Paradiso*. They have an *ironia* of their own. Shakespeare during the last period is comparatively relaxed. He makes a toy of thought. Drawing on the full richness of his inner life, sporadically, as they do, executed with the unanxious brilliance of the maestro who has never lost his flair for improvisation, as they are, the final plays are for all that adjusted to the level of entertainment, controlled by an intention 'which was to please'.

The 'resurrection' scene in *Pericles*, for example, follows immediately on the storm and Thaisa's committal to the sea. The casket in which Thaisa has been placed is washed ashore near the house of Cerimon. Cerimon, as the Epilogue says, is a 'reverend' example of 'learned charity': as Mr. Wilson Knight has pointed out, Shakespeare's first sketch for Prospero.[16] Cerimon prefers the power which wisdom gives to that which the mere governor can exercise:

I held it ever,
Virtue and cunning were endowments greater
Than nobleness and riches: careless heirs
May the two latter darken and expend;
But immortality attends the former,
Making a man a god. 'Tis known I ever
Have studied physic. (III. ii. 26–32)

With a kind of endearing *pietas* Shakespeare builds up his scene along lines slightly old-fashioned. We are shown Cerimon first in actual fact helping 'some Persons who have been shipwrecked'. We then see him being greeted by two gentlemen who announce his character:

Your honour hath through Ephesus pour'd forth
Your charity, and hundreds call themselves
Your creatures, who by you have been restor'd.
(III. ii. 43–5)

Finally Thaisa's coffin is brought in and opened, and the moment of her resuscitation occurs. Again the lyrical note is struck. The verse quickens and pants with wonder:

Gentlemen,
This queen will live: nature awakes; a warmth
Breathes out of her . . . see how she 'gins to blow
Into life's flower again . . .
. . . She is alive; behold
Her eyelids, cases to those heavenly jewels
Which Pericles hath lost,
Begin to part their fringes of bright gold;
And diamonds of a most praised water
Do appear, to make the world twice rich. Live,
And make us weep to hear your fate, fair creature,
Rare as you seem to be!
THAISA. *O dear Diana!*
Where am I? Where's my lord? What world is this?
(III. ii. 92–106)

When thinking of symbolism we must remember that one of the most important things an apple can mean is simply itself. Thaisa's re-awakening feels to her like a rebirth—and also like a loss. To the spectators it is wonder enough, the more so that Thaisa is a miracle of beauty. But the moment attains its highest significance, I think, when it is brought into relation with Pericles' great speech before the committal, and into the general romance frame of 'doutous fortune' and the Providence that smiles while it seems to frown. We do not need to make it more important than that—nor less. And indeed, while there is a restoration of the seeming dead to breathing warmth, it is still a world of trial and of separation to which Thaisa is brought back. Cut off from Pericles, she must retire to Diana's temple and endure her exile in patience.

Diana is the tutelary goddess of the Last Plays. She stands for that chastity which puts its seal on romantic love and which is a reflection of the Virtue that controls and transforms 'base affection' in the *Arcadia*. Thaisa herself is never seen in action as the invincible virgin-mind. That role is reserved for her daughter Marina, and Act IV is devoted to its display.

Recent commentators have argued that Shakespeare's technique in the Last Plays can best be regarded as a development towards symbolism. It is more accurate, I think, to regard the development as a move not towards the symbolic but towards the schematic—the schematic with one addition: Shakespeare imposes on the characters schematically conceived what we have called a *voice*. In Act IV the schematic quickly shows itself. Cleon and Dionyza who have been entrusted with the upbringing of Marina have a daughter of their own, and Dionyza, growing jealous of Marina, determines to have her murdered. The conception is a romance common-place. The 'voice', however, is quickly supplied—Marina entering 'with a basket of flowers' on her way to strew her nurse's grave, and saying:

Ay me! poor maid,
Born in a tempest, when my mother died,
This world to me is like a lasting storm
Whirring me from my friends (IV. i. 17–20)

—and Marina speaking to her would-be murderer the almost monosyllabic language of the heart:

'Why will you kill me?'
'To satisfy my lady'
'Why would she have me killed?
Now, as I can remember, by my troth
I never did her hurt in all my life.
I never spake bad word, nor did ill turn
To any living creature; believe me, la,
I never kill'd a mouse, nor hurt a fly;
I trod upon a worm against my will,
But I wept for it.' (IV. i. 70–9)

—or Marina again speaking in outraged contempt to the pimp in the brothel to which the pirates who rescued her from her murderer have sold her:

Thou hold'st a place, for which the pained'st fiend
Of hell would not in reputation change;
Thou art the damned doorkeeper to every

Coystril that comes enquiring for his Tib,
To the choleric fisting of every rogue
Thy ear is liable, thy food is such
As hath been belch'd on by infected lungs. (IV. vi. 178–184)

Unfortunately for this last voice of strained and schematically violent indignation, Shakespeare suddenly remembers the poor pimp Marina is addressing. He gives him a voice too. Looking out shrewdly from Boult's bleared and piggy eye he makes him say:

What would you have me do? go to the wars, would you? Where a man may serve seven years for the loss of a leg, and have not money enough in the end to buy him a wooden one? (IV. vi. 185–9)

and at once the scene opens out on to other and larger vistas: on to the world whose presiding deities are Mars and Venus, the world of wars and lechery, glamourizable in *Antony and Cleopatra*, despicable in *Troilus and Cressida*, and (for a moment) arrestingly pitiable now in the plight of this Mitylene stews-attendant. Boult is the only person in the play who asks an awkward question that cannot be answered out of the Arcadian book and for the moment it seems as if Shakespeare has broken his own wicket. Boult's question is out of place in the plays of the Last Period as it would not be earlier. The facts of Mars and Venus cannot be considered in them along with the theories of Diana.

Virginity (it is insisted on again in *Cymbeline*, *A Winter's Tale*, and *The Tempest*) is, however, a subordinate item in the whole system, like marriage against one's parents' wishes. How schematic it is can be realized by comparing the handling in Shakespeare's final plays with the treatment in the *Arcadia*. Sidney's exposition is full and he is at pains to relate it to the main moral issues he is concerned about. Chastity in the *Arcadia* is assailed from within and without. The lovers realize its significance between themselves, and the princesses maintain it in captivity against both the arguments of Cecropia and the physical assaults of the three brothers who are left in command when Amphialus becomes a casualty. In *Pericles* it is patience in adversity which is the dominating *motif*, and in Act V patience returns to hold the stage.

The supposed death of his daughter is the second blow Pericles has sustained. It almost exhausts his reserves of 'manliness' but not quite:

He bears
A tempest, which his mortal vessel tears,
And yet he rides it out. (IV. iii. 29–31)

Pericles arrives eventually at Mitylene and there, by fortune, his daughter is brought on board his ship in the hope that she will charm him out of his lethargy. Pericles bids her tell her story:

Report thy parentage. I think thou said'st
Thou had'st been toss'd from wrong to injury,
And that thou thought'st thy griefs might equal mine,
If both were open'd . . .
. . . Tell thy story;
If thine consider'd prove the thousandth part
Of my endurance, thou art a man, and I
Have suffer'd like a girl; yet thou dost look
Like Patience gazing on kings' graves, and smiling
Extremity out of act. (V. i. 131–41)

And from now on the scene begins to move again with the urgent, panting life of restoration, wonderment, and an overflowing joy. Pericles is assured at last that it is Marina indeed:

O Helicanus! strike me, honour'd sir;
Give me a gash, put me to present pain,
Lest this great sea of joys rushing upon me
O'erbear the shores of my mortality,
And drown me with their sweetness. O! come hither,
Thou that begett'st him that did thee beget;
Thou that wast born at sea, buried at Tarsus,
And found at sea again. O Helicanus!
Down on thy knees, thank the holy gods as loud
As thunder threatens us; this is Marina . . .
. . . I embrace you. (V. i. 192–223)

Give me my robes. I am wild in my beholding.
O heavens! bless my girl. But, hark! what music?
Tell Helicanus, my Marina, tell him
O'er, point by point. (v. i. 224–7)

The speech transforms the 'humming water' into a 'great sea of joys', and the near-loss of consciousness here is the reverse of that in the former speech, an ecstasy instead of an apathy. Nothing remains but for Thaisa to be found too. When this happens (and Shakespeare crowds the second discovery quickly upon the first) the joy is greater, as Chaucer would say, 'than was the revel of hir mariage'. It is a note similar to that at the end of the *Clerkes Tale* which Shakespeare sounds:

No more, you gods! your present kindness
Makes my past miseries sport: you shall do well
That on the touching of her lips I may
Melt and no more be seen. O! come, be buried
A second time within these arms. (v. iii. 40–4)

* * *

There can be little doubt that in *Pericles* Shakespeare is responding richly—and with almost lyrical excitement—to the inward theme of the Romance. It is the inwardness that is important: the externals alone would never explain either Shakespeare's excitement or the individuality of his accent even when he is handling material that might otherwise be dismissed as merely conventional or 'in the sources'. The tempests of the last plays are Sidneian tempests, too, but that makes them no less Shakespearean.

In *Pericles* Shakespeare has crossed the threshold of the final period. *Pericles* (the last three acts) is the swiftest and most lyrically conceived handling of the romance matter. For one thing, it concentrates on a single aspect only, a single turn of the wheel in the life of a prince who loses wife and daughter and finds them again. The plays that follow *Pericles* are more complex than this, draw on more of the matter, have more than one centre of focus. The most complicated of the later plays is *Cymbeline*, which follows immediately after *Pericles*. Imogen has all the characteristics of the Arcadian heroine. She combines the ideally virginal with the erotically exciting, and we are reminded of the similar combination in Philoclea, whom Pyrocles sees bathing. Like Diaphantus in the *Arcadia* she dresses as a boy and goes to seek her lover. Imogen is the militantly heroic maiden: like Marina's, her chastity is not maintained in a cloister. Then, too, she shares with Pamela that degree of wilfulness which determines her on following her own choice in love rather than submitting to her father's will, and with Philoclea that degree of self-abandonment in love which makes her utterly Posthumus's. Finally, like Philoclea again, and like Cordelia, she has her moment when she is seen as the embodiment of patience: and Shakespeare catches the idiom of the *Arcadia* to express it:

Nobly he yokes
A smiling with a sigh, as if the sigh
Was that it was, for not being such a smile;
The smile mocking the sigh, that it would fly
From so divine a temple, to commix
With winds that sailors rail at.'
'I do note
That grief and patience rooted in him, both
Mingle their spurs together'
'Grow patience!' (IV. ii. 51–8)

But it is in Posthumus that patience has to be brought to birth, after an initially tempestuous falling-away from patience, reason, and love, and after contrition and imprisonment. The vision which Posthumus sees in prison is a little moral interlude on the theme of patience. Jupiter when he appears quotes the appropriate text:

Whom best I love I cross; to make my gift
The more delay'd, delighted. (V. iv. 101–2)

—and so on. The simple world of Guiderius and Arviragus (secured against the corruptions of the Court but frustrating to the instinct of active virtue which possesses them), such detail as Pisanio (the good servant who will not commit the crime his master orders), or the uxorious king and the dissembling queen

—there is little in the play that cannot be paralleled in the *Arcadia*.

At the same time there is surprisingly little in the later plays if we have regard merely to their separable parts which is not implied or foreshadowed in Shakespeare's own work before 1608. A double relationship, therefore, has to be explained: the relation of Shakespeare to what we might call the Sidneian, and the moral continuity which does in fact bind the later plays to the earlier.

It has always been felt that the plays of the last period reveal a Shakespeare in some sense or other 'on the heights'. The most recent interpretations, as we have suggested, stress the element of rebirth and resurrection, the paradisal mood that seems to be expressed. Dr. Tillyard insists on the continuity of the later with the earlier plays.[17] He explains the difference of mood as the result of a shift of emphasis inside an inclusive pattern: the tragic pattern, where, in spite of sorrow and catastrophe, there is nevertheless in the end a suggestion of reconciliation. In the last period, Dr. Tillyard claims, Shakespeare developed the element of reconciliation without altogether losing sight of the darker sides of experience which make that reconciliation significant. The view I have implied would agree that there is a real continuity between the religious vision of *Lear* and the schematic presentations of the final period. I suggest, however, that the resolutions taking place are not simply resolutions based on the exaggeration of one formal element in the tragic pattern. I see them, rather, as differences of stress inside a particular and inclusive moral scheme. The link between the tragedy of *King Lear* and the romance of *Pericles* is patience and what patience implies. The moral scheme behind the whole of Shakespeare's work is more inclusive and more integrated than we have been apt to suppose. The new lyricism of wonder and reconciliation, for example, has sometimes been used as the basis for arguing that after 1606 (or after *Timon*) Shakespeare underwent some inner change—had a breakdown, or a religious experience. But once the moral continuity is recognized, there is not the same necessity to assume nervous breakdown or religious illumination in between writing *Timon* and *Pericles*. *King Lear* in fact can be regarded as a study in patience unrewarded although achieved, *Timon* and the Roman plays as studies in impatience, and the plays of the last period as studies in patience rewarded. Shakespeare is turning from one part to another of a unified field. A change of taste in the audience, a tiredness in the writer himself—any of a number of secondary causes would equally account for the shift of subject matter, without compromise to Shakespeare's integrity or his sincerity. Shakespeare does have his growing points—if we like, his 'conversions'. There are in his plays thresholds of insight that are crossed, leading to a deepening of moral insight and an increased lucidity in his moral world, the full and inclusive lucidity which, I think, Shakespeare achieved in *King Lear*. The vision is personal from one point of view. From another it is quite impersonal. It is Shakespeare's personal recognition of features in a moral landscape which are still in our day (as they were when he wrote) public, not dependent on Shakespeare's will. Shakespeare is not a romantic devising a system of his own to prevent his enslavement by that of another man. This public landscape is that of Storm and Adversity, and of Virtue, and Patience, and Charity —a landscape shaped and weathered by the general Christian tradition of the west from Boethius onwards, shaped too (immediately) by the contemporary literary means of depicting this landscape in the Romance.

When, however, we stress the continuity of the late plays and the plays of the great tragic period we should not omit to observe too the essential differences between plays such as *King Lear* and plays such as *A Winter's Tale* or *The Tempest*. Professor D. G. James has distinguished well between work where the Imagination predominates and work where the Intelligence is mainly involved, between work which seems to offer symbols and that which hands over formulae.[18] *King Lear* he maintains is a work of imaginative and symbolic force. Using Professor James's distinction we might describe the plays of the final period as works in which formula, and schema, and intelligent manipulation, are the dominant things. Up to 1606 Shakespeare was growing. His works are an existential record of his growth. After that time all his work seems to be that of a man who has got things finally clear and is no longer worried. Not only are things clear, they are almost cut and dried. Shakespeare now can engage or disengage himself just as far as he wishes. He can be unanxious, he can even be careless. All the time, certainly, he can preserve that attitude which Sidney Greville called *ironia.* The danger of Sidney as opposed to Hollinshed was simply that the adoption of his scheme meant the adoption of an inclusive set of answers to carefully prepared questions—and this alters the whole tone of the work based on Romance.

And the tone is as important as the matter for a proper assessment of the last plays. How is Shakespeare placed in regard to them? What is his attitude to himself in the act of writing? How can the literary intention be weighed?—I have myself no doubt that the last plays are less serious than those of the tragic period. *King Lear* is a religious statement. *The Tempest* is not. *King Lear* we should never call *beautiful.* Any one of the last plays, in almost every act, compels just that adjective from us: we are taken by beauty continually. The last plays are the fancies of Lear dreaming of Cordelia refound. They exist at a remove from reality. They give us a schema for life rather than the life itself.

We might now turn back to Shakespeare's maturest work, to Shakespeare's own statement of the theme traditional to Christian piety whether Catholic or Reformist, Shakespeare's personal handling of Patience perfected. *King Lear* is evidence of the breadth and depth of the spirituality in the popular tradition. The play has an older play behind it. Behind that again is the folk-tale. This is one aspect of it. On another side, it incorporates part of the Plexirtus saga from the *Arcadia,* the Greek names of the original vigorously Englished into Edgar, and Edmund, and Gloster. Shakespeare was aware too of Spenser's handling of the story. It was the *Faerie Queene* (the other Great House epic) that helped Shakespeare to the final form of Cordelia's name. Again, Shakespeare's play is in a line that goes back to the gravest and most measured of Chaucer's Tales—itself a rendering of Petrarch's version of the widespread Griselda story. Finally, of course, *King Lear* culminates a development of Shakespeare's mind as well as of his art. It supplies a touchstone whereby, I think, the greatness or less-greatness of the plays that follow can most readily be measured.

CHAPTER FOUR

King Lear and Christian Patience: A Culmination

Mr. T. S. Eliot has suggested that the clues to Shakespeare's working philosophy might well be looked for not in Machiavelli or Montaigne but in the Stoicism which the Renaissance revived and made current.[1] It would seem rather that what has often been taken for Stoicism in Shakespeare is not Stoicism at all but more simply the orthodox teaching on Christian Patience. I propose to glance at the placing of this Christian virtue first in Chaucer, secondly in the sixteenth-century Reformers Becon, Hutchinson, and Coverdale; finally at its exemplification in *King Lear*—sometimes cited as the most obviously heathen of Shakespeare's tragedies:

> *As flies to wanton boys, are we to the gods;*
> *They kill us for their sport.* (IV. i. 36–7)

At the outset a half-concession to the classics might be made. The teaching of the heathen philosophers was always recognized as chiming in on occasion with that of the Bible. Where the two coincided Seneca or Cicero or Aristotle would always be enlisted as supporting authorities. Bacon in his essay *Of Adversity*, for example, quotes Seneca and then comments that it is 'speech . . . much too high for a heathen'. Bacon deprecated so near an approach by ordinary reason to the kind of wisdom we expect more from revelation. In *A Spiritual and Most Precious Pearl* [illegible]verdale quotes Aristotle, the Stoics, Cicero, and Seneca as cl[illegible]cal witnesses to the value of patience in adversity: 'wise and [illegible]e heathen men, which we call philosophers, among whom this was a common proverb and sentence: "Bear and forbear".'[2] Coriolanus and Antony are given as clear examples of defective patience. The one carried arms against his country, the other committed suicide: 'The very reason of man can discern and judge, that such things are against nature, and against all virtue and honesty.'—And then Coverdale proceeds to distinguish clearly between heathen and Christian patience. His distinction is similar to that found in Roger Hutchinson: 'The heathen and philosophers profess a certain kind of sufferance, in that they regard not the grievous chances of this life . . . but they lacked the patience that God esteemeth, and is commended to us in Christ's example.'[3] Finally, we might go back to Chaucer who reflects the mediaeval sources of this sixteenth-century pastoral wisdom. In *The Persones Tale* Chaucer holds up the supreme example of Christian patience:

'Heeragayns suffred Crist ful paciently, and taughte us pacience, whan he bar upon his blissed shulder the croys, up-on which he sholde suffren despitous deeth. Heer may men lerne to be pacient; for certes, noght only Cristen men been pacient for love of Jesu Crist, and for guerdoun of the blisful lyf that is perdurable; but certes, the olde payens, that nevere were Cristene, commendeden and useden the vertu of pacience.'[4]

Patience nowadays is thought of as a negative thing. It is a mood of blank and empty passiveness when we put up with ourselves and our afflictions because there is nothing else to do. Throughout the Middle Ages, and as far down at least as Henry More's *Enchiridium Ethicum*, patience was the opposite of this. Instead of being negative it was positive. Instead of being a void it was a condition filled with the richest graces of the Christian life. Roger Hutchinson tried to indicate this richness and repletion. His image unfortunately is a culinary one: 'We must not only be patient in trouble, but also our patience must be garnished with certain properties.'[5] This richness of content, then, must be remembered all the time by the modern reader of Chaucer or Coverdale or Shakespeare. On the other side Christian patience is different from the Stoical patience (also an active and willed condition) by reason of the difference of content between the two. Stoic patience is an impassive withstanding of all that conflicts with Reason. At best it is indifference, at worst unfeelingness. Christian patience is in contrast with this patience, too—and the contrast was never overlooked by anyone during the Renaissance years. Writing on the Passion of Christ Coverdale affirms, for example:

'The patience therefore of Christians standeth not in this, that they feel no passion, or be not fearful, heavy, or sorry; but in this, that no cross be so great, as to be able to drive them away from Christ. Yea, the more the cross that God the Father hath laid upon them doth make them to smart, and the more it presseth them (so that they bear it), the more precious and more excellent is their patience; which patience we ought to declare, but not as they that suffer or feel no passion at all.'[6]

Modern patience, then, is emptied of content and significance: it amounts to sitting still and doing nothing. Stoic patience rests on impassive reason. Christian patience is based on faith and suffering charity. It expresses the sum of the Christian virtues. Its supreme example is the activity of Christ dying on the Cross: 'a marvellous stedfastness of patience . . . to perform the redemption of mankind.'[7]

Bearing these two distinctions in mind—the essential opposition of Christian patience both to the impassiveness of the Stoics and the blank passiveness of modern resignation—we can turn to a closer examination of patience as defined by the Middle Ages and the sixteenth century.

Patience ranked extremely high among the virtues. Christ was its perfect exemplar, Christ's Passion its supreme manifestation. Patience in fact is an inclusive term for the whole range of virtues linked and integrated and displayed in the central mystery of the Cross. How inclusive it is may be seen in the advice of Prudence enjoining patience on Melibeus. The *Tale of Melibeus* portrays the Job-like trial of a man by adversity and his Christian triumph through listening to the good advices of his wife. Melibeus learns to be patient and to forgive his enemies. The turning point is when he listens to Prudence's homily. The text for that homily might well have been the verse Prudence quotes from 'Seint Jame in his epistle: that "patience is a great vertu of perfeccioun".'[8]

We are always to understand that 'in mannes sinne is every manere of ordre or ordinance turned up-so-down'.[9] Patience is the sign and guarantee that man is not assenting to such a topsy-turvydom. Patience is the will holding on through faith to the belief that reality is really rightside-up, in spite of appearances and seeming contradictions. Patience connotes faith in God's goodness and obedience to His law: the law enjoining love of God, love of ourselves, and love of our neighbour as ourself. It is reason withstanding the test of evidential contradiction, and charity withstanding the temptations of affliction. It is this that gives it such inclusiveness. To hold on to patience is to grasp the one necessary life-line.

This conception of patience as an inclusive virtue accounts for its recurrence throughout *The Parsones Tale* as the grand prophylactic against sin. Pride, for example, the first of the Deadly Sins, reveals itself in impatience. Patience presumably would be a sovereign remedy. Envy, the second of the Sins, often springs from impatience. The passage in which Chaucer makes the appropriate definitions is important. It begins to explain:

As flies to wanton boys are we to the gods:
They kill us for their sport.

The backbiting of Envy sometimes:

'springeth of impacience agayns god, and sometime agayns man. Agayns god it is, whan a man grucceth agayn the peynes of helle, or agayns poverte, or los of catel, or agayn reyn or tempest; or els grucceth that shrewes han prosperitee, or elles for that good men han adversitee. And alle thise thinges sholde men suffre paciently, for that they comen by the rightful judgment and ordinance of god.'[10]

But it is against Wrath that patience is especially effective, because wrath—the natural reaction of the flesh against attack or encroachment or any diminution of the self whatever—is the prime temptation of adversity. Patience however

'is a vertue that suffreth swetely every mannes goodnesse, and is nat wrooth for noon harm that is doon to him. The philosophre seith, that "pacience is thilke vertu that suffreth debonairely alle the outrages of adversitee and every wikked word". This vertu maketh a man lyk to god, and maketh him goddes owene dere child, as seith Crist. This vertu disconfiteth thyn enemy.'[11]

Whenever patience is the theme nothing short of the maximum seems to be claimed for it. The virtue that 'maketh a man lyk to god' is the strongest reminder of the God of the Old Testament who bore with the follies of His people, and of the God of the New Testament who suffered the cross.

Chaucer's most famous exemplification of patience, of course, is *The Clerkes Tale*. The story of the Patient Griseld is one of his most deceptively simple and most cunningly wise achievements. It is a story apt to fall very flat with a modern reader. Our difficulty, ironically enough, is that we fall into impatience. And our impatience is the exact measure of our lack of insight into Chaucer's meanings and of our failure to appreciate the deliberate strain on our patience which Chaucer is imposing: deliberately imposing, I suggest, on the evidence of the Envoy Chaucer affixed to the story. Part of his audience was the Wife of Bath. And Griselda, like Beatrice, Chaucer knew to be not of this earth:

Grisilde is deed, and eek her pacience,
And bothe atones buried in Itaille;
For which I crye in open audience,
No wedded man so hardy be t'assaïlle
His wives pacience, in hope to finde
Grisilde's, for in certein he shall faille.[12]

And Chaucer returns himself from his story to the realm of the unregenerate, his readers.

The modern reader fidgets to interfere between the husband and the patient wife he is putting to such shameful test. Chaucer on the other hand, with magnificent understanding of what he is doing, never once questions the rightness of everything that happens in the story. Behind the story, of course, for the Middle Ages, is the trial of Job by Satan—and Job's victory; or the trial of the Saint by God through adversity—and the Saint's reward. What the Middle Ages would readily recognize as the allegorical meaning of the poem is just this: Griselda is the soul and the husband is God. Anagogically (that is, applying the story to things heavenly) Griselda is the Church suffering tribulation and Walter is the Church's spouse. This is the framework into which the story fits. The trials of Griselda are cruel. But the cruelty is merely a trial. And no such trials can break down Christian patience. It is all therefore part of a divine and loving comedy. Invincible patience is assured of the crown. The joy of Griselda and Walter in their reunion at the end of the story is grander and more sumptuous

Than was the revel of hir mariage.[13]

The trial of perfect patience is bound to have a happy ending. Our impatience is wrong: it means we have not realized the nature of the contestants nor the terms of the contest. *The Clerkes Tale* is Chaucer's Book of Job:

This storie is seyd, nat for that wyves sholde
Folwen Griselde as in humilitee,
For it was importable, though they wolde;
But for that every wight, in his degree,
Sholde be constant in adversitee
As was Grisilde; therfor Petrark wryteth
This storie, which with heigh style he endyteth.

For, sith a woman was so pacient
Unto a mortal man, wel more us oghte
Receyven all in gre that god us sent;
For greet skile is, he preve that he wroghte.
But he ne tempteth no man that he boghte,
As seith Seint Jame, if ye his pistel rede;
He preveth folk al day, it is no drede,

And suffreth us, as for our exercyse,
With sharpe scourges of adversitee
Full ofte to be bete in sondry wyse;
Nat for to know our wil, for certes he,
Ere we were born, knew al our freletee;
And for our beste is al his governaunce;
Lat us than live in vertuous suffraunce.[14]

Before leaving Chaucer's handling of the virtue patience we might look at the one person in the poem who exemplifies impatience. This is Griselda's father. When Griselda returns home apparently disgraced and destitute he

Curseth the day and tyme that nature
Shoop him to been a lyves creature.[15]

In other words (if we might over-emphasize where Chaucer merely hints) the impatient man does not recognize adversity as coming from God. Nor does he retain faith in God. Nor does he even acknowledge God to be his creator. His existence he ascribes to 'nature', and wishes he had not been born. All these are mortal sins and heathenish offences.

* * *

'Prosperity', Bacon wrote, 'is the blessing of the Old Testament; adversity is the blessing of the New, which carrieth the greater benediction, and the clearer revelation of God's favour.' Bacon's jauntiness compares badly with Chaucer's wise and sympathetic sobriety of tone. The content of Bacon's remark, however, he inherits from the Middle Ages. It is handed down to the Elizabethans through any number of preachers and divines.

In Thomas Becon's exposition of *The Catechism* it is laid down that God tempts us two manner of ways.[16] The first temptation is that of prosperity, the second adversity. Of the two prosperity is the more dangerous. Afflictions are of God, and as many as He loves He chastens. We must 'obediently, patiently, and thankfully bear and suffer whatever cross, trouble, and sickness, persecution, or any other kind of adversity God layeth upon us'. The grand example of patience is Jesus, who bore adversity 'without any murmuring or grudging against God'. Other examples are Job, Tobias 'whom God deprived of his sight, that he might try his patience', and David who was 'grievously and mortally pursued of his ungodly and disobedient son Absolon'. (Gloucester in *King Lear* carries the double load of both Tobias's and David's afflictions.) In adversity the chief temptation is that men will 'with impatience murmur and grudge against the Lord God, yea, and blaspheme his holy name'. To be proof against the temptation we must 'surrender and give up to Him ourselves, our wills, our affections, our lusts, that . . . his most godly and blessed will may be done in us'. Again the grand positive conception of patience comes through. The surrender of our will is not a negative thing: it means that God's will henceforth will act through us.

Roger Hutchinson's *Two Sermons of Oppression, Affliction, and Patience* fill in more details of the same picture.[17] Afflictions are of two sorts, and two kinds of patience are required according as our miseries are deserved or undeserved. Prosperity corrupts. Hutchinson agrees with Becon that adversity is safer. Adversity, in fact, is a stern but well-meaning tutor: rather rough on a man, but you can't help approving of him, and you feel all the better after you've been through his hands. He is 'Master Adversity . . . our overseer and governor' by God's appointment, 'and as long as any uncleanness, any spot of sin shall remain in us, he will never cease, but will continually trouble and buffet us'. Like Becon, too, Hutchinson is aware that adversity 'causeth them to blaspheme God, maketh men desperate'. Patience alone is proof against it, and patience furthermore is the key to all the virtues. 'True Christian patience is not vain-glorious, is not void of faith, is associate with humility, is powdered and salted with obedience to all God's commandments, is garnished with hope of the life to come.' The culinary image returns but Hutchinson manages to suggest the positive richness and full savour of this patience which sounds so like a satisfying meal. He means what Chaucer put more delicately in *The Tale of Melibeus*: patience is the Reason of Aquinas joined to the Charity of St. Paul. For Hutchinson as well as for Chaucer, Christ, 'a pattern and a mirror of all virtue', is also the supreme exemplar of patience. Impatience is all sins in one: 'impatience causeth idolatry, causeth murder, brought in rebellion and unthriftness, expelled from heaven, and banished out of paradise.'[18]

Tantalizing Shakespeare echoes come and go in the pages of the divines. We have already encountered Coriolanus and Antony linked together in the same sentence as men of defective patience. Hutchinson's 'pattern . . . of all virtue' is another phrase from a patience context. It is still some distance from Lear's 'I will be the pattern of all patience: I will say nothing.' But intermediate links might be supplied from the Elizabethan Homilies.

In the *Sermon of the Passion for Good Friday* as in *The Parsones Tale*, Christ's behaviour is held up as 'a most perfect example of all patience and sufferance'.[19] In the same sermon patience (as in Hutchinson) is equated to charity, and in the same passage occurs the missing half of Lear's phrase:

'Perfect patience careth not what or how much it suffereth, nor of whom it suffereth, whether of friend or foe; but it studieth to suffer innocently and without deserving. Yea, he in whom perfect charity is careth so little to revenge, that he rather studieth to do good for evil, according to the example of our Lord Jesus Christ, who is the most perfect example and pattern of all meekness and suffrance.'[20]

Lear's phrase sounds like a flowing together of the phrases from the Homily. It is not necessary to assume that Shakespeare read widely among the divines: there is of course no evidence that he did not. The Homilies in any case gather up most of the thoughts and many of the turns of phrase of the divines. They suggest the medium whereby the teaching of the theologians on patience might have come to Shakespeare's notice.

If Shakespeare did read the divines on the subject of patience one possible source-book at least would be Coverdale's translation from the German of Otho Wermullerus, *The Spiritual and Most Precious Pearl*. The pearl, of course, is 'the noble and precious virtue called patience'.[21] The book is a manual for the Christian in adversity. As such it is more exhaustive than Hutchinson or Bacon, though they have already mapped some of the ground.

It contains, I think, everything we need in order to understand Shakespeare's handling of adversity as displayed in the reactions to adversity of Cordelia, Lear, Gloucester, and Edgar.

In adversity we are to remember that God may have sent the troubles for our sins. And there is a significant tit-for-tat in the punishments: 'God tempereth and frameth the punishment even like unto the sin, so that they do both agree together as well in form and likeness, as in proportion and quality.'[22] Or, as Edgar says to Edmund:

> *The Gods are just, and of our pleasant vices*
> *Make instruments to plague us:*
> *The dark and vicious place where thee he got*
> *Cost him his eyes.* (v. iii. 172–5)

Afflictions, however, proceed from God's fatherly regard to our correction. Furthermore, they sort out the wheat from the chaff. (This is a point especially significant in relation to the theme of *King Lear*.) Judas is indistinguishable from the other disciples until the testing time of adversity arrives. And similarly, in adversity we not only get to know the truth from the perfect imitation in others, we also come the better to know ourselves. Prosperity blinds us, adversity opens our eyes: we stumble when we see. In adversity we recognize our own weakness so that we turn to God in prayer for His assistance. We are softened by adversity. We are led to penitent self-examination. Fortitude and temperance, meekness and love, patience and compassion—these are the fruits of adversity: 'The cross, adversity, maketh a man soft, tame, patient, sober, loving, and friendly, both towards himself and towards all other also.'[23]

The ungodly do not benefit from adversity. On the contrary, they 'rave and rage', fall into despair, give themselves over to the devil, and commit suicide. They mistake the origin and purpose of adversity, ascribing it not to God but to Fortune:

'The unfaithful do ascribe their prosperity and felicity to their own working, wisdom, and policy, and not to God: and their misfortune and adversity they ascribe to blind fortune, as though fortune had a certain power to work herself, without the working of God.'[24]

So the impatient man blasphemes and turns on God:

'he imagineth with himself nothing else, but that God is utterly wroth and displeased with him; and can find in his heart to curse and blaspheme God, as though he were a cruel, unmerciful, and unrighteous God.'[25]

To avoid all this, in adversity we must be patient, as God Himself is patient:

'And God doth not only command patience, but also is himself patient and long-suffering; which destroyeth not at once the whoremonger, and extortioner, and other such like wicked and damnable people with a lightning or thunderbolt, although his holy and strait righteousness requireth no less. He giveth time and space sufficient for the man to repent, and to return to grace again.'[26]

We must not charge God foolishly. We must pray. We must make amendment of life. We must not give way to fits of depression: 'utterly resist and banish all manner of heavy, sorrowful, and desperate fancies and imaginations of the mind.'

A Spiritual and most Precious Pearl runs over all the familiar ground. Here and there it adds its own particular inflection. One last quotation might be made, which will return us—with a difference—to the point from which this account of patience set out. We began by noting the external difference between Christian patience and Stoic impassiveness. The divines maintained this. At the same time they upheld a distinction internal to Christian patience, and one which could easily be mistaken for Stoicism of a new variety. This is the distinction between the patience that is natural and the patience that is of faith. The two together supply the full framework in which to set Shakespeare's *King Lear*: for Shakespeare knew of this distinction, too.

'There are two kinds of hope; the one is of nature, and the other cometh of faith. The natural hope is a special gift and benefit of God, which after a certain manner doth help and comfort a man that is troubled and vexed, that he does not utterly despair; but in the midst of all adversity, hopeth that in a while it will, within a while, be better, and so waiteth and tarrieth till the adversity be overblown.

'Now if this natural hope have such a strength and virtue, should not the other hope, which the spirit of God doth newly inspire through faith, work a much greater and perfecter patience and strength . . . ? And although the natural hope doth often and many times fail and deceive, and is always uncertain, yet this christian hope doth never fail nor deceive.'[27]

* * *

Of the four people in *King Lear* who exhibit reactions to adversity within the traditional scheme two show patience and two defective patience. The group is meticulously balanced. Cordelia is the perfection of Christian patience that suffereth long and is kind. Her father is an instance of extreme falling-off—first into rage and then into madness. Gloucester and Edgar occupy a middle region between these two limits. The son is steadily patient. The father wavers on the edge of grace and despair and is only saved in the end by the ministrations of his son. Adumbrated in the Shakespearian pattern are Coverdale's two spheres of nature and spirit.

Cordelia is conceived in the same terms as Chaucer's Griselda. She stands in the light of the same clear Christian tradition. It is the dazzle of this halation which has made everybody since Shakespeare's time (Victor Hugo excepted) so dim when they have spoken about her. The discussion of her conduct in the first scene is a good example. Almost everyone has strained to detect in her the traces of her father's pride. We might equally well, I suggest, discuss Griselda's long-sufferance as disguised self-interest or peasant stupidity. Cordelia, when she says nothing is the sheep before the shearers that must be dumb. She is quite simply the truly patient woman and daughter. If we recall Coverdale's 'patience . . . of Christians' we can see clearly the relation between his abstract description and Shakespeare's living presentation. Cordelia has that patience which does not exclude passion—the passion of grief and the passion of compassion:

KENT. *Did your letters pierce the Queen to any demonstration of grief?*

GENTLEMAN. *I say she took them, read them in my presence,*
And now and then an ample tear trill'd down
Her delicate cheek, it seem'd she was a Queen
Over her passion, who most revel-like,
Sought to be King o'er her.

KENT. *O then it moved her.*

GENTLEMAN. *Not to a rage, patience and sorrow strove*
Who should express her goodliest, you have seen
Sunshine and rain at once, her smiles and tears
Were like a better way: those happy smilets,
That play'd on her ripe lip seem'd not to know,
What guests were in her eyes which parted thence,
As pearls from diamonds dropp'd; in brief,
Sorrow would be a rarity most beloved,
If all could so become it. (IV. iii. 12–26)

Throughout the play Cordelia is the model of perfect patience and the charity it connotes. The habitual terms applied to her in the play would be extravagant in respect of a mere woman. They are quite natural when applied to a woman who is conceived as a Griselda or a Beatrice.

Lear, at the beginning of the play, is quite obviously the man whom prosperity has corrupted. Furthermore, Nature in him stands on the very verge of her confine. He labours therefore under a double handicap. Adversity finds him unprepared.

When Goneril first crosses him he flies into a rage. Albany cries, 'Pray sir be patient!' but he is not listening. When he meets Regan, however, he has had time to recall the advice. To his elder daughter he says:

Mend when thou canst, be better at thy leisure,
I can be patient, I can stay with Regan,
I and my hundred knights. (II. iv. 231)

And when Regan disappoints him of this:

but for true need,
You heavens give me that patience, patience I need!
(II. iv. 273–4)

Lear's course throughout the play is punctuated now with efforts to retain patience and constant failures to do so. Even after the admission of his true need he calls on the gods to fool him not so much 'to bear it tamely'. He would have 'noble anger' and inexpressible revenge.

He is on the Heath and already strained to breaking point when he says:

No, I will be the pattern of all patience,
I will say nothing. (III. ii. 37–8)

—recalling by his words the pattern behaviour of Cordelia in Act I, Scene i, as well as the more august examples. And the struggle continues. Lear is brought to Christian repentance and compassion in his prayer on the Heath, only to be submitted immediately to the ensuing strain which makes him mad. In his madness he 'raves and rages' like the impatient man of Coverdale. But even in the madness Shakespeare keeps within the traditional bounds and does not speak at random. Lear's anarchism in his madness is the Anabaptist heresy as Roger Hutchinson reckons it, a perversion of compassion. Should a Christian refuse to go to law with another Christian? Hutchinson asks, and gives one possible reply:

' "Aye," saith Master Anabaptist, "for Christ our Master, whose example we must follow, he would not condemn an advoutress woman to be stoned to death according to the law, but shewed pity to her. . . . He *non dominatus sed passus*; would be no magistrate, no judge, no governor." '[28]

Lear's words are antinomian in the same sense:

'change places, and handy-dandy, which is the Justice, which is the thief . . . thou might'st behold the great image of authority, a dog's obeyed in office . . . why dost thou lash that whore? . . . None does offend, none, I say none.' (IV. vi. 157–173)

He sees Gloucester (now blinded) standing beside him as his rage finishes. There is a sudden change of mood. The madness now picks up the teaching of Christian patience to mix in with its other impertinencies. It is one of the most powerful ironies in the play:

If thou wilt weep my fortunes, take my eyes,
I know thee well enough, thy name is Gloucester:
Thou must be patient; we came crying hither:
Thou know'st the first time that we smell the air
We wawl and cry. I will preach to thee: mark.

(IV. vi. 181–5)

Cordelia and Lear are the opposite extremes. Edgar and Gloucester, I think, are conceived in less elevated terms. They can be regarded as exemplifying natural honesty and natural hope. As such, of course, they still come within the sphere covered by patience—patience the Christian rather than the heathen virtue.

Edgar is a complicated figure. The complication is increased by the changes of mask he adopts in his transactions with the various adversities he meets. His quality is to bend and not to break, to devise a folding of virtue that will counter the pleatings of cunning. His supreme wisdom is 'Ripeness is all'—a phrase that struck a rich premonitory chord in Mr. T. S. Eliot. He is Poor Tom, horned devil, ministering angel, simple rustic, mysterious champion, and finally English king. The disguises rapidly symbolize, among other things, the triumph of natural hope and natural patience. Edgar's uncomplaining long-sufferance from the point when he decides he will

with presented nakedness outface
The winds, and persecutions of the skies (II. iii. 11–12)

to the point when he can even 'exchange charity' with the brother who has been his enemy is exemplary. His bearing and forbearing is rewarded at last, and by one of those natural miracles of patience, for

Nothing almost sees miracles
But misery. (II. ii. 172–3)

In between these two points he has had to withstand successfully the serial temptations of adversity.

Edgar feels the special stroke of adversity when he meets with his father. At the beginning of Act IV, Scene i, he has attained the stable mood which can find consolation in the thought that when one is down one cannot fall. It is the consolation of 'natural hope' that 'in a while it will, within a while, be better':

Yet better thus, and known to be contemn'd
Than still contemn'd and flatter'd; to be worst,
The lowest and most dejected thing of Fortune,
Stands still in esperance, lives not in fear:
The lamentable change is from the best,
The worst returns to laughter. Welcome then,
Thou unsubstantial air that I embrace:
The wretch that thou hast blown unto the worst,
Owes nothing to thy blasts. (IV. i. 1–9)

This is the mood of the Duke in Arden. In *King Lear* it exists only to be shattered. The blinded Gloucester is led on by the Old Man. Edgar cries out:

O Gods! Who is't can say I am at the worst?
I am worse than e'er I was. . . .
And worse I may be yet: the worst is not,
So long as we can say this is the worst. (IV. i. 25–8)

The patience that can be complacent is not yet perfect. The sweets of positive charity and compassion have not yet been pressed from it.

Gloucester, whom we see now, is a figure already purged and improved by affliction. His first words show him considering others rather than himself, and he dismisses the Old Man. His next epitomize the wisdom expounded in *A Spiritual and Most Precious Pearl*:

I have no way, and therefore want no eyes:
I stumbled when I saw. Full oft 'tis seen
Our means secure us, and our mere defects
Prove our commodities. O dear son Edgar,
The food of thy abused father's wrath;
Might I but live to see thee in my touch
I'ld say I had eyes again. (IV. i. 18–24)

Prosperity corrupts and is more dangerous than adversity, and 'like as prosperity shutteth and blindeth the eyes of men, even so doth trouble open them'. Gloucester is seen 'more tame, patient, sober, loving, and friendly, both towards all other also'. He knows himself better. He is penitent and would make amendment of life.

Yet Gloucester's patience is not without deficiency. He wavers this side and that—though without the violence of Lear's extremeness—crossing the line dividing hope from despair, faith from unfaith. He can 'find it in his heart to curse and blaspheme God, as though he were a cruel, unmerciful, and unrighteous God'. The puritan language is maybe too strong to apply to what Gloucester actually says, but

As flies to wanton boys are we to the Gods,
They kill us for their sport

is certainly 'murmuring and grudging'.

In spite of this, charity works in the afflicted man, as Coverdale says it will. Gloucester gives his purse to Poor Tom:

Here take this purse, you whom the heaven's plagues
Have humbled to all strokes: that I am wretched
Makes thee the happier: Heavens deal so still:
Let the superfluous and lust-dieted man,
That slaves your ordinance, that will not see
Because he does not feel, feel your powers quickly:
So distribution should undo excess,
And each man have enough. (IV. i. 65–72)

Gloucester's course over the Heath is lit repeatedly from within by this light of Christian patience, as Lear's is only once on the magnificent occasion of his all-embracing prayer. Lear's course describes wider zigzags than Gloucester's, and has more sudden contrasts. Immediately after his prayer, for example, Lear is precipitated into madness, doomed to 'rave and rage'. Madness is impatience made absolute. The flawed patience of Gloucester has the result which, in the divines, is complementary to madness. He suffers from the defect rather than from the excess of energy. His temptation is not to defy God and fight, but to give over and die: the temptation of suicide. There is a beautiful

October melancholy, a rich tiredness, in the words he meant to be his last:

> *O you mighty Gods!*
> *This world I do renounce, and in your sights*
> *Shake patiently my great affliction off:*
> *If I could bear it longer, and not fall*
> *To quarrel with your great opposeless wills,*
> *My snuff and loathed part of nature should*
> *Burn itself out. If Edgar live, O bless him:*
> *Now fellow, fare thee well.* (IV. vi. 35–42)

The jump from the cliff, of course, is a trick of Edgar's. And it is by an innocent deception that Gloucester is persuaded a miracle has happened. Even at this point Coverdale has a sentence that falls in with Shakespeare's conception:

'a great weight and substance of the matter dependeth and hangeth on this point, that a man conceive a right judgment and opinion of all things that happen and chance. For everything appeareth so unto us, even as we in our thoughts and minds do fancy, imagine, and conceive it.'[29]

'Think,' says Edgar.

> *Think that the clearest Gods, who make them honours*
> *Of men's impossibilities, have preserved thee.* (IV. v. 74–5)

And, of course, it might be that Edgar's deception is the means taken by the clearest Gods to intervene. In the realm of real spiritual advancement the end justifies the means. Gloucester henceforth, at any rate, is saved from despair:

> *I do remember now: henceforth I'll bear*
> *Affliction, till it do cry out itself*
> *Enough, enough, and die. That thing you speak of,*
> *I took it for a man: often 'twould say*
> *The Fiend, the Fiend; he led me to that place.*
> EDGAR. *Bear free and patient thoughts.* (IV. v. 76–81)

Lear enters at this point, and now on the stage together are the two complements of impatience, the one preaching to the other, 'Thou must be patient'.

Gloucester is constantly in danger of relapse, of falling into 'all manner of heavy, sorrowful, and desperate fancies and imaginations of the mind'.[30] Edgar has to rally him:

What in ill thoughts again? Men must endure
Their going hence, even as their coming hither,
Ripeness is all: come on. (v. ii. 9–11)

'Ripeness' is a profound word as Edgar uses it here. All its meanings in terms of the play and of Shakespeare's growth and development up to 1606 cannot be gone into here. We can see, at least, that it points to a cycle in human affairs. It suggests processes that man cannot with safety either hasten or cut short. It tacitly recommends acceptance. What we must accept is something we might call, however vaguely, 'Nature'. There is no overt Christian reference, except that to see the course over the Heath as a process leading to the fulfilment of a beneficent design, the fruition of some ultimately healthful purpose, argues an act of faith which no Senecan would feel to be justified by the facts. The Nature which ripens man through adversity is, by implication, the Christian rather than the heathen thing.

In Gloucester's case, as in Lear's, there is a strong impression of ripeness and fulfilment in the end. The fruit that falls at last from the bough is rich and full and sweet. Gloucester has exhausted the curve of despair, and he has seen in Lear the great fire of rage burn itself out. What finally kills him is neither rage nor despair, but the opposite of these—such a tension between joy and compassion as breaks his heart:

in this habit
Met I my father with his bleeding rings,
Their precious stones new lost: become his guide,
Led him, begg'd for him, sav'd him from despair.
Never (O fault) reveal'd myself to him,
Until some half-hour past when I was arm'd,
Not sure, though hoping of this good success.

I asked his blessing, and from first to last
Told him our pilgrimage. But his flaw'd heart
(Alack too weak the conflict to support)
'Twixt two extremes of passion, joy and grief,
Burst smilingly. (v. iii. 190–201)

Gloucester's death is a death in the very throe of patience—of that Christian patience which is a positive fullness, an active state, a condition in which the great forces of repentance and reconciliation are compounded. 'Smilingly' indicates the crowning gift that adversity has brought. It takes us back to the ending of *The Clerkes Tale*:

Thus hath this pitous day a blisful ende:
For every man and woman dooth his might
This day in murthe and revel to dispende
Til on the welkne shoon the sterres light.
For more solempne in every mannes sight
This feste was, and gretter of costage,
Than was the revel of hir marriage.

CHAPTER FIVE

Antony and Cleopatra: A Shakespearian Adjustment

At each stage in his development Shakespeare displays a surprising capacity for renewal. Let us assume that *Antony and Cleopatra* comes after *King Lear*, that it goes with *Coriolanus*, and that both it and *Coriolanus* immediately precede the so-called 'last period'. Between *Antony and Cleopatra* and the plays that have gone before there is no obvious connection in theme or technique. At the same time, only Plutarch links it with *Coriolanus*. Nothing in it would normally prepare us for *Cymbeline* or *The Winter's Tale* to follow. This apparent isolation is one of the main obstacles to a correct focus on the play. There seems to be a break in the internal continuity of the Shakespearian series—a continuity of series which stretches, I think, from *Henry VI* to *King Lear* at least, and which could possibly be extended to include *Timon*: though here again there is something of a lesion, and special factors, external to the 'inner biography' of Shakespeare as a playwright, might have to be invoked to explain all that is happening. *Timon*, however, it might be granted, is the aftermath of *King Lear*. Can the same be said about *Antony and Cleopatra*?

I

To describe the swiftness of *Antony and Cleopatra* we need to draw on the imagery of the cinema. There is more cinematic movement, more panning, tracking, and playing with the camera, more mixing of shots than in any other of Shakespeare's tragedies. At the same time the technique is always under deliberate, almost cool, control. *Antony and Cleopatra* has none of the haphazardies of *Pericles* nor any of the plot-imposed vagaries of the last period. The technique is inwardly related to the meaning Shakespeare has to express. What is indicated is not enervation or indifference, but rather what Coleridge recognized as 'giant power', an 'angelic strength'.

The swift traverse of time and space has often been commented upon. There is also the mixing. Egypt is called up vividly in Rome by Enobarbus's descriptions. Rome is always felt as a real presence in Egypt. On the frontiers of Empire Ventidius discusses what repercussions his victories will have on the people at staff-headquarters. Equally the present is interpenetrated by the past. Antony's past, particularly, is always powerfully put before us:

Antony,
Leave thy lascivious wassails. When thou once
Wast beaten from Modena, where thou slew'st
Hirtius and Pansa, consuls, at thy heels
Did famine follow, whom thou fought'st against
Though daintily brought up, with patience more
Than savages could suffer; thou didst drink
The stale of horses, and the gilded puddle
Which beasts would cough at; thy palate then did deign
The roughest berry on the rudest hedge;
Yea, like the stag, when snow the pasture sheets,
It is reported thou didst eat strange flesh,
Which some did die to look on. (I. iv. 55–68)

So, too, is Cleopatra's:

I found you as a morsel cold upon
Dead Caesar's trenchar; nay, you were a fragment
Of Cneius Pompey's; besides what hotter hours,
Unregister'd in vulgar fame, you have
Luxuriously pick'd out. (III. ix. 116–20)

The hinterland of the quarrels that alternately divide and bring together again the triumvirate is constantly being suggested, troubles, truces, and manœuvres that go back (like Cleopatra's love-affairs) to Julius Caesar's days. In no other of his plays is Shakespeare at such pains to suggest the stream of time past and its steady course through the present. In the public world of Roman affairs this is especially so. In the other world of Cleopatra the same suggestion of perspective always frames what is said and done. Is Antony merely the last of a long succession of such lovers? Or is this affair singular and unique as all love-affairs claim to be? Not enough weight has been given in recent assessments of the play to the ambiguity which invests everything in Egypt equally with all things in Rome. Yet this ambiguity is central to Shakespeare's experience in the play. If it is wrong to see the 'mutual pair' as a strumpet and her fool, it is also wrong to see them as a Phoenix and a Turtle.

In addition to the swiftness and the variety of the impacts, and the interpenetration of the parts of time and space as they mix in the speech of the people immediately before us, there is also the added burden which Shakespeare's 'giant power' of compelling presentation imposes. The effects are at once those of a rapid impressionism and a careful lapidary enrichment. Each figure, however minor, has its moment when it comes up into the brilliant foreground light—the Soothsayer with his 'infinite book of secrecy', the Old Man wishing 'much joy o' the worm', Enobarbus describing the barge on the Nile, Lepidus asking 'What manner o' thing is your crocodile?' Ventidius giving once for all the field-officer's view of the higher-ups, the Eunuch and the game of billiards, Dolabella, Octavia, even Fulvia whom we never see: the canvas seems covered with Constable's snow.

Another feature of Shakespeare's technique which makes for the impression of uniqueness might be pointed to here. Shakespeare seems to be innovating also in methods of character-portrayal. Some of the stage conventions, as described by Miss Bradbrook, do not seem to apply. Which, for example, are we to believe—what Caesar says about Antony after he is dead, or what he says about him, and his conduct towards him, while he is alive? What was Fulvia's 'character', about whom we have such conflicting reports? Throughout the play we are forced by Shakespeare himself not to take comment at its face value.

Judgments are more personal here than elsewhere. Goneril and Regan discussing their father's condition are reliable judges. Caesar, Antony, Enobarbus, the soldiers Demetrius and Philo, are not—or not to the same extent. Judgment knits itself back into character as it might do in Ibsen, and character issues from a mutable and ambiguous flux of things. Antony's momentary *agnorisis* can be generalized to cover the whole play:

> *Sometimes we see a cloud that's dragonish;*
> *A vapour sometimes like a bear or lion,*
> *A tower'd citadel, a pendant rock,*
> *A forked mountain, or blue promontory,*
> *With trees upon't, that nod unto the world*
> *And mock our eyes with air: thou hast seen these signs;*
> *They are black vespers pageants . . .*
> *That which is now a horse, even with a thought*
> *The rack dislimns, and makes it indistinct*
> *As water is in water . . .*
> *My good knave, Eros, now thy captain is*
> *Even such a body: here I am Antony,*
> *Yet cannot hold this visible shape, my knave.*
>
> (IV. xii. 2–14)

There is something deliquescent in the reality behind the play. It is a deliquescence to the full display of which each judgment, each aspect pointed to, and each character, is necessary, always provided that no single one of these is taken as final. The proportion of comment and judgment on the central characters is higher in *Antony and Cleopatra* than anywhere else in Shakespeare. This further underlines its uniqueness and the difficulties of coming by an adequate final assessment. Antony and Cleopatra are presented in three ways. There is what is said about them; there is what they say themselves; there is what they do. Each of these might correspond to a different 'level' of response. Each is in tension against the others. Each makes its continuous and insistent claim on the spectator for judgment in his own right. The pigments vividly opposed to each other on the canvas have to mix in the spectator's eye.

Underlying, however, the bewildering oscillations of scene,

the overlapping and pleating of different times and places, the co-presence of opposed judgments, the innumerable opportunities for radical choice to intervene, there is, I think, a deliberate logic. It is this which gives the play its compact unity of effect and makes its movement a sign of angelic strength rather than a symptom of febrility. It is the logic of a peculiarly Shakespearian dialectic. Opposites are juxtaposed, mingled, married; then from the very union which seems to promise strength dissolution flows. It is the process of this dialectic—the central process of the play—which we must trace if we wish to arrive anywhere near Shakespeare's meaning.

II

The first scene opens with Philo's comment on the 'dotage' of his general:

those his goodly eyes
That o'er the files and musters of the war
Have glow'd like plated Mars: now bend, now turn
The office and devotion of their view
Upon a tawny front; his captain's heart,
Which in the scuffles of great fights hath burst
The buckles on his breast, reneges all temper,
And is become the bellows and the fan
To cool a gipsy's lust. (I. i. 2–10)

Nothing more has time to be said. Antony and Cleopatra themselves appear. Their first words express the essence of romantic love, a tacit contradiction of all that Philo seems to have just suggested:

CLEO. *If it be love indeed, tell me how much.*
ANT. *There's beggary in the love that can be reckon'd.*
CLEO. *I'll set a bourn how far to be belov'd.*
ANT. *Then must thou needs find out new heaven, new earth.*
(I. i. 14–17)

Again immediately, an attendant announces the arrival of news from Rome. The atmosphere of the Egyptian court changes. We see the opposite effects of the intrusion on the two it most concerns. Antony will not hear the messengers. Cleopatra insists that he shall. Antony is taunted with a wicked caricature of what the news might be, and of the relation in which he stands to Rome. Yet the version is sufficiently like to make Antony blush—from anger, or shame, or both:

Your dismission
Is come from Caesar; therefore hear it, Antony,
Where's Fulvia's process? Caesar's would I say? both?
Call in the messengers. As I am Egypt's queen,
Thou blushest, Antony, and that blood of thine
Is Caesar's homager; else so thy cheek pays shame
When shrill-tongued Fulvia scolds. (I. i. 26–32)

Antony's reaction is to pitch his romantic vows higher still, asserting his independence of Rome in terms that should leave no doubt as to where he stands:

Let Rome in Tiber melt, and the wide arch
Of the rang'd empire fall! Here is my space.
Kingdoms are clay; our dungy earth alike
Feeds beast as man: the nobleness of life
Is to do thus; when such a mutual pair
And such a twain can do't, in which I bind
On pain of punishment, the world to weet
We stand up peerless. (I. i. 33–40)

This again has all the ring of absolute and heroic self-committal. Cleopatra's reply, however, is typical both of herself and of the ambivalence that runs through everything in the play:

Excellent falsehood!
Why did he marry Fulvia and not love her?
I'll seem the fool I am not; Antony
Will be himself. (I. i. 40–3)

Her first words might be oxymoron or plain disbelief. The next call up the vista of Antony's past, with its broken pledges and unconscious insincerities—if they were no more. Her last words are highly ambiguous and turn the whole situation upside-down: she is the helpless creature wilfully blinding and deceiving herself, Antony is the self-contained and calculating manipulator of her weaknesses. In replying, Antony is like the man innocent of ju-jutsu who thinks he is pushing when really he is being pulled:

But stirr'd by Cleopatra.
Now, for the love of Love and her soft hours,
Let's not confound the time with conference harsh . . .
. . . What sport tonight? (I. i. 43–7)

Shakespeare gives the operative lines a subtle falsity of note that could equally indicate hearty play-acting, slightly awkward self-consciousness, or wilful evasion. Cleopatra's answer is realist and comes with a new urgency:

Hear the ambassadors. (I. i. 48)

It drives Antony also to something we can recognize as more fully himself—something that is perceptive and tinged with the masterful as well the reckless:

Fie, wrangling queen!
Whom everything becomes, to chide, to laugh,
To weep; whose every passion fully strives
To make itself in thee fair and admir'd.
No messenger, but thine; and all alone,
Tonight we'll wander through the streets and note
The qualities of people. Come, my queen;
Last night you did desire it: speak not to us.
(I. i. 48–55)

This is not only Antony's view of Cleopatra's character, and a reliable account of what she is really like. It is also an expression of the deliquescent reality at the heart of the play which incarnates itself most completely in the persons of the hero and heroine. After Antony's speech, with this two-fold authority it bears, the comment of the soldiers seems peculiarly limited and out of place:

DEM. *Is Caesar with Antonius priz'd so slight?*
PHIL. *Sir, sometimes when he is not Antony,*
He comes too short of that great property
Which still should go with Antony.

DEM. *I am full sorry*
That he approves the common liar, who
Thus speaks of him at Rome; but I will hope
Of better deeds tomorrow. (I. i. 56–62)

It serves to remind us, however, of the world that stands around the lovers, the world of the faithful soldier who can only understand the soldierly, the world of 'the common liar' that enjoys the unpleasant 'truth', the world, too, of Rome and Caesar that is radically opposed to the world of Egypt and Cleopatra.

The first scene is only slightly more than sixty lines long. Yet it is sufficient to illustrate all the main features of the play we have pointed to, and extensive enough to set up the swinging ambivalence—the alternatives and ambiguities constantly proposed to choice—which will govern and control our whole reaction to the play. There is the speed and oscillation, the interpenetration of Rome and Egypt and of present and past. Above all there is the dialectic marriage of the contraries and their dissolution through union. The jealousy of Cleopatra towards Fulvia, the outrage of Caesar to Antony's *amour propre*—these negative repulsions can serve to hold the mutual pair together as firmly as positive attractions. Antony and Cleopatra are opposed to the world that surrounds and isolates them. In this isolation their union seems absolute, infinite, and self-sufficient. Yet the war of the contraries pervades the love, too. In coming together they lapse, slide, and fall apart unceasingly.

The outstanding achievement of the first scene is the way in which it begins with the soldiers' condemnation and returns us at the end to the same thing—allowing for this side eighteen lines out of the sixty-two. Yet at the end we are no longer satisfied as to the adequacy of what Demetrius and Philo say. Not that what they say has been disproved by what we have seen of Antony and Cleopatra. They are and they remain a strumpet and her fool. To have any judgment at all is to choose, apparently, either the judgment of the soldiers at the beginning of the scene or the lovers' own self-assessment that immediately follows it. (Coleridge chose the former; Dr. Sitwell and Mr. Wilson Knight take the latter.) To entertain either judgment, however, is not enough. The deliquescent truth is neither in them nor between them, but contains both. *Antony and Cleopatra* is Shakespeare's critique of judgment.

Scene i played out romantic love and lovers' quarrels on a lofty stage. It also gave the sharp local comment of the soldiery. Scene ii takes the theme of love below-stairs and changes key. It also gives the universal comment of the Soothsayer, with its suggestion that everything is already decided, the tragedy is in the nature of things, now is already over, the future past, the present always:

> *In nature's infinite book of secrecy*
> *A little can I read . . .*
> *I make not but foresee. . . .*
> *You have seen and prov'd a fairer former fortune*
> *Than that which is to approach.* (I. ii. 11–36)

In place of the 'romance' of love, Charmian, Iras, and Alexas give the 'reality'. The reality in this case is a strong succession of rich, powerful, and adequate males:

'Let me be married to three kings in a forenoon, and widow them all; let me have a child at fifty to whom Herod of Jewry may do homage; find me to marry with Octavius Caesar, and companion me with my mistress.'

It reads like a parody of Cleopatra's aspirations, just as the women's bickering and teasing of Alexas mimics Cleopatra's handling of Antony:

'Alexas—come, his fortune, his fortune. O! let him marry a woman that cannot go, sweet Isis, I beseech thee; and let her die too, and give him a worse; and let worse follow worse, till the worst of all follow him laughing to his grave, fifty-fold a cuckold!'

This seems a nightmare version of Antony's fate—the reflection in a distorting mirror of the thoughts and feelings that course through Antony after Cleopatra's desertion in the disastrous sea-fight.

The group is interrupted in its fortune-telling by the entry of

Cleopatra. She is looking for Antony. Her remarks prepare us for the different mood about to establish itself:

> *Saw you my lord? . . .*
> *He was disposed to mirth; but on the sudden*
> *A Roman thought hath struck him.* (I. ii. 86–91)

Antony is heard approaching. Cleopatra immediately goes off. Now that he is coming she will refuse to see him.

When Antony appears he is surrounded by the messengers from Rome and immersed in Roman affairs. He veers savagely to the point of view both of the soldiers in the first scene and 'the common liar' in Rome. Throughout the play this is what marks him off from Cleopatra and makes him a more complex meeting-ground for the opposites than even she is herself. He can understand and respond to the appeal of Rome as much as he can understand and respond to Egypt:

> *Speak to me home, mince not the general tongue;*
> *Name Cleopatra as she's called in Rome;*
> *Rail thou in Fulvia's phrase; and taunt my faults*
> *With such full licence as both truth and malice*
> *Have power to utter. O! then we bring forth weeds*
> *When our quick winds lie still; and our ills told us*
> *Is as our earing. Fare thee well awhile . . .*
> *These strongly Egyptian fetters I must break,*
> *Or lose myself in dotage.* (I. ii. 113–126)

The second messenger brings news of Fulvia's death. It is characteristic of the play that what is hated during life should find favour once it is dead. Later in this scene that is reported to be the case with Pompey in the popular reaction to him:

> *our slippery people—*
> *Whose love is never link'd to the deserter*
> *Till his deserts are past—begin to throw*
> *Pompey the great and all his dignities*
> *Upon his son.* (I. ii. 198–202)

This is what happens, too, in Antony's case when, once he is dead, Octavius sings his praises. It also happens when Cleopatra is thought to have committed suicide and Antony flings from vituperation to acclamation almost without pausing. It happens now with Fulvia. Antony says:

> *There's a great spirit gone! Thus did I desire it:*
> *What our contempts do often hurl from us*
> *We wish it ours again; the present pleasure,*
> *By revolution lowering, does become*
> *The opposite of itself: she's good being gone.*
> *The hand could pluck her back that shov'd her on.*
> *I must from this enchanting queen break off.*
>
> (I. ii. 131–7)

Typically, when he joins the general, Enobarbus summons all the counter-arguments. To leave Egypt would be to kill Cleopatra. 'She is cunning,' Antony says, 'past man's thought.' 'Alack, sir, no,' Enobarbus rejoins,

'her passions are made of nothing but the finest part of pure love. We cannot call her winds and waters sighs and tears; they are greater storms and tempests than almanacs can report: this cannot be cunning in her; if it be, she makes a shower of rain as well as Jove.' (I. ii. 156–62)

Even if we read Enobarbus's words as irony, the double-irony that works by virtue of the constant ambivalence in the play still turns them back to something approaching the truth: and Cleopatra's real distress and anxiety over Antony's departure have already cut through the scene like a knife. The ding-dong continues:

ANTONY. *Would I had never seen her!*
ENOBARBUS. *O, sir! you had then left unseen a wonderful piece of work.*
ANTONY. *Fulvia is dead.*
ENOBARBUS. *Sir?*
ANTONY. *Fulvia is dead.*
ENOBARBUS. *Fulvia?*
ANTONY. *Dead.*
ENOBARBUS. *Why, sir, give the gods a thankful sacrifice . . . this grief*

is crown'd with consolation; your old smock brings forth
a new petticoat. (I. ii. 163–181)

Antony, however, has made up his mind to go back to Rome.

Antony does go back to Rome—but not in the mood and not with the motives of thorough-going reformation in which he remains at the end of Scene ii. In Scene iii the alchemy of the Shakespearian process is further at work. It works to make Antony do the thing resolved upon but for reasons the very opposite of those which led him to the resolve. The scene of his departure is chosen for Cleopatra's most sincere avowal. Having tormented Antony beyond all bearing she suddenly breaks off with:

Courteous lord, one word.
Sir, you and I must part, but that's not it;
Sir, you and I have loved, but there's not it;
That you know well: something it is I would—
O my oblivion is a very Antony
And I am all forgotten. (I. iii. 86–91)

Antony's final words in the scene almost catch the very idiom of *The Phoenix and the Turtle:*

Let us go. Come.
Our separation so abides and flies,
That thou, residing here, go'st yet with me,
And I, hence fleeting, here remain with thee.
Away! (I. iii. 101–5)

It is, so to speak, the honeymoon of the contraries—only possible while the lovers are apart.

III

The first three scenes show how pervasive is that quality in technique and vision which we have called the Shakespearian 'dialectic'. It comes out in single images, it can permeate whole speeches, it governs the build-up inside each scene, it explains the way one scene is related to another. The word 'dialectic', of course, is unfortunately post-Hegelian. The thing we wish to point to, however, in using the word, is Shakespearian. In *Antony and Cleopatra* Shakespeare needs the opposites that merge, unite, and fall apart. They enable him to handle the reality he is writing about—the vast containing opposites of Rome and Egypt, the World and the Flesh.

Rome is the sphere of the political. Shakespeare uses the contraries (long before Blake) to give some sort of rational account of the irrationals there involved. The common people, for example, is 'the common liar'. Antony has already noted that its love is 'never link'd to the deserver till his deserts are past'. Caesar, too, has his own cold knowledge of the same fact:

It hath been taught us from the primal state
That he which is was wished until he were;
And the ebb'd man, ne'er loved till ne'er worth love,
Comes dear'd by being lack'd. This common body,
Like to the vagabond flag upon the stream,
Goes to and back, lackeying the varying tide,
To rot itself with motion. (I. iv. 41–7)

The great men, however, behave exactly as they say the commons do, too. With Antony, Fulvia becomes dear'd by being lack'd. In Caesar's case it is the same. The threat of Pompey makes him suddenly appreciate the grandeur of Antony's leadership, courage, and endurance. The magnanimous praise of Antony in Act V is only possible because Antony by then is dead. The law is general: judgment is a kind of accommodation to the irrational on reason's part:

men's judgments are
A parcel of their fortunes, and things outward
Do draw the inward quality after them,
To suffer all alike. (III. ix. 31–4)

Even soldierly 'honour' is rooted in the ambiguous. When Pompey's man mentions his treacherous scheme for disposing of all Pompey's rivals at one blow (the rivals are also Pompey's guests on board ship), Pompey exclaims:

Ah, this thou should'st have done
And not have spoken on't. In me 'tis villainy;
In thee 't had been good service. Thou must know
'Tis not my profit that does lead mine honour;
Mine honour it. Repent that e'er thy tongue
Hath so betray'd thine act; being done unknown,
I should have found it afterwards well done,
But must condemn it now. (II. vii. 80–7)

The law is general because it reflects the nature of the terrene world—the tidal swing of the opposites on which all things balance in a motion that rots them away.

The self-destruction of things that rot with the motion which their own nature and situation dictate is almost obsessive with Shakespeare throughout the play. The political world is the manipulation of the common body they despise by the great men whom the commons can never love until they are safely rid of them. The pattern which remains constant in all the possible groupings is that of open conflict alternating with diseased truce, neither of them satisfactory:

Equality of two domestic powers
Breeds scrupulous faction. The hated, grown to strength,
Are newly grown to love. . . .
And quietness, grown sick of rest, would purge
By any desperate change. (I. iii. 47–54)

Compacts between the great men merely represent the temporary sinking of lesser enmities in front of greater:

lesser enmities give way to greater.
Were't not that we stand up against them all
'Twere pregnant they should square amongst themselves.
(II. i. 43–5)

Pompey's is a correct appreciation. It is because of him that Octavius and Antony are reconciled. They will rivet the alliance by means of Antony's marriage to Caesar's sister. Enobarbus knows automatically that this union is a certain way of making conflict ultimately inevitable.

'you shall find the bond that seems to tie their friendship together will be the very strangler of their amity.' (II. vi. 7–9)

Octavia is one of Shakespeare's minor triumphs in the play, beautifully placed in relation to the main figures and the tenor of their meaning. Her importance is apt to be overlooked unless her careful positioning is noted. Her presence gives a symmetrical form to the main relations of the play. Octavia is the opposite of Cleopatra as Antony is the opposite of Caesar. She is woman made the submissive tool of Roman policy where Cleopatra always strives to make the political subservient to her. (It is the thought of being led in triumph by Caesar as much as the thought of Antony's death which finally decides Cleopatra for suicide.) Where Caesar and Cleopatra are simple and opposite, Octavia—like Antony—is a focal point for the contraries. There is nothing in her as a 'character-study' to account for the effect her presence has. It is rather that she is transparent to the reality behind the play and one of its least mistakable mediators. On the occasions when she appears herself, or when mention is made of her, it is the interfluent life of this reality rather than the personality of its vehicle which fills the scene.

Her first entry is significant. It comes immediately after the triumvirate and Pompey have made their pact. We have just heard the following satiric account of Lepidus's behaviour—and Lepidus, like Octavia, has to stand between the two demi-Atlases:

AGRIPPA. *'Tis a noble Lepidus.*
ENO. *A very fine one. O! how he loves Caesar.*
AGRIPPA. *Nay, but how dearly he adores Mark Antony.*
ENO. *Caesar? Why, he's the Jupiter of men!*
AGRIPPA. *What's Antony? the god of Jupiter.*
ENO. *Spake you of Caesar? How, the nonpareil!*
AGRIPPA. *O Antony! O thou Arabian bird!* (III. ii. 6–12)

Then the triumvirate and Octavia come on. Octavia stirs Antony deeply. But the imagery in which his vision of her is clothed carries us past the person described to the 'varying tide' by which everything in the play is moved:

Her tongue will not obey her heart, nor can
Her heart obey her tongue; the swan's down feather
That stands upon the swell of the full tide
And neither way inclines. (III. ii. 47–50)

Octavia never escapes from her position midway between the contraries that maintain and split the world. With Antony away in Athens, her brother first falls on Pompey then finds a pretext to destroy Lepidus. He is now ready to mount his attack on the last remaining rival, his 'competitor in top of all design'. Hearing of it, Octavia cries:

A more unhappy lady,
If this division chance, ne'er stood between,
Praying for both parts. . . .
. . . Husband win, win brother,
Prays and destroys the prayer; no midway
'Twixt these extremes at all. (III. iv. 12–20)

Octavia's is the alternative plight to Cleopatra's for womanhood in the play. The choice is merely between alternative methods of destruction—either at one's own hands, or through the agency of the process. The 'swan's down feather', like the 'vagabond flag', can only swing on the tide until it rots with motion.

Rome is the world of politics and policy. Its supreme term is Octavius Caesar himself. He, like Octavia, must be brought into relation with the pattern which he helps in part to define. Half his significance is lost if he is seen only as a 'character'. In Octavius's case we have aids external to the play which help towards a clear focus on what Shakespeare intends by him. He falls recognizably into Shakespeare's studies of the 'politician'—the series that begins with Richard III and continues down through Edmund.

Octavius is a notable development in the figure which started as a machiavel pure and simple. Shakespeare now betrays no sign of alarm, no hint of revulsion or rejection, almost no trace of emotion in putting him into a story. He is taken completely for granted. He has arrived and he will stay. He is part of the structure of things. He is 'Rome'. In matters of politics and policy it is obvious that only the politicians count: and politics is one half of life. The politician is a perfectly normal person. Given all his own way he would doubtless bring—as Octavius is certain his triumphs eventually will bring—a 'universal peace'. To be normal like him, of course, and to enjoy the peace he offers, two conditions are necessary. First, one must sacrifice the other half of life; then, one must be prepared to make complete submission. By the time Shakespeare comes to depict Octavius he has refined away all the accidentals from the portrait—the diabolism, the rhetoric, the elaborate hypocrisy, the perverse glamour: everything but the essential deadliness and inescapability. Octavius marks an advance on Goneril and Regan. He shares their impatience with tavern and brothel. He has no share in the lust which entraps even them. We might almost doubt whether Octavius has any personal appetite at all, even the lust for power. His plan to lead Cleopatra in triumph has the appearance of a desire for personal satisfaction, but it is more likely that it fits into an impersonal wish on Caesar's part to subdue all things to Rome. Caesar, of course, is Rome—but a kind of impersonal embodiment. He is more like a cold and universal force than a warm-blooded man. He is the perfect commissar, invulnerable as no human being should be. Egypt has no part in his composition.

Caesar has the deceitfulness of the machiavel, but he plays his cards without any flourish. He can rely on his opponents to undo themselves: they are more complicated than he. He puts the deserters from Antony in the van of his own battle:

Plant those that are revolted in the van,
That Antony may seem to spend his fury
Upon himself. (IV. vi. 9–11)

The strength and weakness of those ranged against him constitute Caesar's fifth column. The opposition will rot away or eat the sword it fights with.

It is in the last act that Egypt and Rome confront each other singly, the duplicity of Caesar pitted against the duplicity of Cleopatra. There is no doubt as to who shall survive the contest. The tension is maintained throughout the fifth act only by the doubt left in the spectator's mind right up to the end as to which way Cleopatra will jump: will she accept submission or will she take her own life? The whole play has prepared us for just this doubt. In a sense, whichever way the decision goes it is immaterial. The point of the play is not the decisions taken but the dubieties and ambivalences from which choice springs—the barren choice that only hastens its own negation. Rome, from the nature of things, can admit no compromise. Egypt, equally, can never submit to its contrary. So Cleopatra kills herself.

Cleopatra has been loved by recent commentators not wisely but too well. As Caesar impersonates the World, she, of course, incarnates the Flesh. Part of Shakespeare's sleight of hand in the play—his trickery with our normal standards and powers of judgment—is to construct an account of the human universe consisting of only these two terms. There is no suggestion that the dichotomy is resolvable: unless we are willing to take the delusions of either party as a resolution, the 'universal peace' of Caesar, the Egypt-beyond-the-grave of Antony and Cleopatra in their autotoxic exaltations before they kill themselves.

Cleopatra is the Flesh, deciduous, opulent, and endlessly renewable:

she did make defect perfection . . .
Age cannot wither her, nor custom stale
Her infinite variety; other women cloy
The appetites they feed, but she makes hungry
Where most she satisfies; for vilest things
Become themselves in her, that the holy priests
Bless her when she is riggish. (II. ii. 239–48)

The Flesh is also the female principle. Cleopatra is Eve, and Woman:

No more but e'en a woman, and commanded
By such poor passion as the maid that milks
And does the meanest chares. (IV. xiii. 73–5)

She is also Circe:

Let witchcraft join with beauty, lust with both!
(II. i. 22)

Shakespeare gives Cleopatra everything of which he is capable except his final and absolute approval. Cleopatra is not an Octavia, much less a Cordelia. The profusion of rich and hectic colour that surrounds her is the colour of the endless cycle of growth and decay, new greenery on old rottenness, the colour of the passions, the wild flaring of life as it burns itself richly away to death so that love of life and greed for death become indistinguishable:

'there is mettle in death which commits some loving act upon her, she hath such a celerity in dying.' (I. ii. 152–4)

The strength of the case Shakespeare puts against her is undeniable. The soldiers, and Caesar, and Antony when the consciousness of Rome speaks through him, are right, as far as they go. The strength of the case for her is that it is only Rome that condemns her. And Egypt is a force as universal as Rome—as hot as the other is cold, as inevitably self-renewing as the other is inescapably deadly. And the only appeal that can be made in the play is from Egypt to Rome, from Rome to Egypt. And neither of these is final, because between them they have brought down Antony, the 'man of men'.

For the tragedy of *Antony and Cleopatra* is, above all, the tragedy of Antony. His human stature is greater than either Cleopatra's or Caesar's. Yet there is no sphere in which he can express himself except either Rome or Egypt, and to bestride both like a Colossus and keep his balance is impossible. The opposites play through Antony and play with him, and finally destroy him. To Caesar (while Antony is in Egypt, and alive) he is:

A man who is the abstract of all faults
That all men follow. (I. iv. 9–10)

To Cleopatra he appears instead a 'heavenly mingle':

Be'st thou sad or merry,
The violence of either thee becomes,
So it does no man else. (I. v. 59–61)

When she sees him returning safe from the battlefield she cries:

O infinite virtue! Com'st thou smiling from
The world's great snare uncaught? (IV. viii. 17–8)

After he is dead she remembers him as a kind of Mars:

His face was as the heavens, and therein stuck
A sun and moon, which kept their course, and lighted
This little O, the earth . . .
His legs bestrid the ocean; his rear'd arm
Crested the world; his voice was propertied
As all the tuned spheres, and that to friends;
But when he meant to quail and shake the orb,
He was as rattling thunder. For his bounty,
There was no winter in't, an autumn 'twas
That grew the more by reaping; his delights
Were dolphin-like, they show'd his back above
The element they lived in; in his livery
Walk'd crowns and crownets, realms and islands were
As plates dropped from his pocket . . .
. . . Nature wants stuff
To vie strange forms with fancy, yet t'imagine
An Antony were nature's piece 'gainst fancy,
Condemning shadows quite. (v. ii. 79–99)

This, of course, is again the past catching fire from the urgent needs of the present, flaring in memory and imagination as it never did in actuality. Antony is nothing so unambiguous as this. The most judicious account of him is that of Lepidus when he is replying to Caesar's strictures:

I must not think there are
Evils enow to darken all his goodness:
His faults in him seem as the spots of heaven,
More fiery by night's blackness; hereditary
Rather than purchased, what he cannot change
Than what he chooses. (I. iv. 10–15)

Here the ambiguities of the play's moral universe get their completest expression: faults shine like stars, the heaven is black, the stars are spots. Ambivalence need go no further.

IV

The earlier criticism of *Antony and Cleopatra* tended to stress the downfall of the soldier in the middle-aged infatuate. More recent criticism has seen the play as the epiphany of the soldier in the lover, and the reassurance of all concerned that death is not the end. In the view that has been put forward here neither of these is right. The meaning of *Antony and Cleopatra* is in the Shakespearian 'dialectic'—in the deliquescent reality that expresses itself through the contraries.

Antony and Cleopatra swims with glamour. Once we lose sight of the controlling structure of the opposites which holds the play together we are at the mercy of any random selection from its occasions. And occasions abound—moments, opinions, moods, speeches, characters, fragments of situation, forked mountains and blue promontories, imposed upon us with all the force of a 'giant power'. It is, then, eminently understandable that critics should succumb like Antony or hold aloof like Demetrius and Philo.

The Roman condemnation of the lovers is obviously inadequate. The sentimental reaction in their favour is equally mistaken. There is no so-called 'love-romanticism' in the play. The flesh has its glory and passion, its witchery. Love in *Antony and Cleopatra* is both these. The love of Antony and Cleopatra, however, is not asserted as a 'final value'. The whole tenour of the play, in fact, moves in an opposite direction. Egypt is the Egypt of the biblical glosses: exile from the spirit, thraldom to the flesh-pots, diminution of human kindness. To go further still in sentimentality and claim that there is a 'redemption' motif in Antony and Cleopatra's love is an even more violent error. To the Shakespeare who wrote *King Lear* it would surely smack of blasphemy. The fourth and fifth acts of *Antony and Cleopatra* are not epiphanies. They are the ends moved to by that process whereby things rot themselves with motion—unhappy and bedizened and sordid, streaked with the mean, the ignoble, the contemptible. Shakespeare may have his plays in which 'redemption' is a theme (and I think he has), but *Antony and Cleopatra* is not one of them.

Antony and Cleopatra is an account of things in terms of the World and the Flesh, Rome and Egypt, the two great contraries that maintain and destroy each other, considered apart from any third sphere which might stand over against them. How is it related to the plays of the 'great period', the period which comes to an end with *King Lear*?

The clue is given, I think, in the missing third term. *Antony and Cleopatra* is the deliberate construction of a world without a Cordelia, Shakespeare's symbol for a reality that transcends the political and the personal and

> *redeems nature from the general curse*
> *Which twain have brought her to.*
> (*King Lear*, IV. vi. 211-2)

One must call the construction deliberate, because after *King Lear* there can be no doubt that Shakespeare knew exactly where he was in these matters. Both *Antony and Cleopatra* and *Coriolanus* follow North's Plutarch without benefit of clergy. Both Antony and Coriolanus were cited by the sixteenth-century moralists as notable examples of heathen men who lacked patience—the one committing suicide, the other rebelling against his country. In *Antony and Cleopatra* suicide is the general fate of those who wish to die. Cleopatra gives the audience a conscious reminder of the un-Christian ethos involved:

> *All's but naught;*
> *Patience is sottish, and impatience does*
> *Become a dog that's mad: then is it sin*
> *To rush into the secret house of death*
> *Ere death dare come to us?* (IV. xiii. 78-82)

The Christian world-view in Shakespeare's time turned round a number of conceptions which were covered by the Elizabethans in their examination of the meanings of 'Nature'. The theme of 'Nature' runs through the whole of *Macbeth*, *King Lear*, and *Timon*. Its absence from *Antony and Cleopatra* suggests Shakespeare's satisfaction that for him the theme is exhausted. He is inwardly free now to look at a classical story, deliberately excise the Christian core of his thought, and make up his account of what then remains over.

This explains the effect, I think, of *Antony and Cleopatra*. Freedom from the compulsive theme of the Natures, the conscious security gained from having given it final expression, enabled Shakespeare to handle something new and something which was bound to be intrinsically simpler. Part of the energy absorbed in grappling with theme now bestows itself on technique. *Antony and Cleopatra* gives the impression of being a technical *tour de force* which Shakespeare enjoyed for its own sake.

The excision also explains, I think, the tone of the play—the sense of ripe-rottenness and hopelessness, the vision of self-destruction, the feeling of strenuous frustration and fevered futility, that which finds its greatest expression in Antony's speech before he gives himself his death-blow:

Now
All length is torture; since the torch is out,
Lie down and stray no further. Now all labour
Mars what it does; yea, very force entangles
Itself with strength; seal then, and all is done.

(IV. xii. 45–9)

The excision, finally, explains what might be regarded as a diminution of scope in *Antony and Cleopatra*. (We are, of course, only comparing Shakespeare with himself.) The theme of Rome and Egypt, however, is simpler than the theme of 'Nature', the trick of using the contraries (again, for Shakespeare) relatively an easy way of organizing the universe. It is unusual, at any rate, for Shakespeare to rely on one trick so completely as he seems to do in *Antony and Cleopatra*. At times we are almost tempted to believe he has fallen a victim of habitual mannerism.

One last comment might be made. We referred at the beginning of this chapter to Shakespeare's surprising capacity for self-renewal. *Antony and Cleopatra* is not the aftermath of Lear in any pejorative sense. There is something in it that is new and exciting and profound. Shakespeare remained still the youngest as the greatest of his contemporaries. In *Antony and Cleopatra* he is making his own adjustments to the new Jacobean tastes. The play is Shakespeare's study of Mars and Venus—the presiding deities of Baroque society, painted for us again and again on the canvasses of his time. It shows us Virtue, the root of the heroic in man, turned merely into *virtu*, the warrior's art, and both of them ensnared in the world, very force entangling itself with strength. It depicts the 'man of men' soldiering for a cynical Rome or whoring on furlough in a reckless Egypt. It is the tragedy of the destruction of man, the creative spirit, in perverse war and insensate love—the two complementary and opposed halves of a discreating society.

For more obvious, if less great manifestations of the same discreating society, interested almost exclusively in love and war (and these both more narrowly conceived and more over-valued emotionally than they ever are by Shakespeare) we must turnto Beaumont.

CHAPTER SIX

Beaumont and Fletcher: Jacobean Absolutists

After all, Beaumont and Fletcher were but an inferior sort of Shakespeares and Sidneys.

C. LAMB, *Specimens of an English Dramatic Poetry.* Note on *Maid's Tragedy*

Charles Lamb's judgment is not likely to be reversed however much the plays of Beaumont and Fletcher are re-read or re-assessed. But something less than justice is done them if the Shakespeare comparison is made prematurely or in the wrong way. In any such comparison they will naturally come out on the wrong side; and they have rarely been read without the motive of comparison in mind. Coleridge, for example, wrote:

'The plays of Beaumont and Fletcher are mere agregations without unity; in the Shakespearian drama there is a vitality which grows and evolves itself from within—a key-note which guides and controls the harmonies throughout.'[1]

And Lamb:

'Fletcher's ideas moved slow; his versification, though sweet, is tedious; it stops every moment; he lays line upon line, making up one after the other, adding image to image so deliberately that we see where they join: Shakespeare mingles everything, he runs line into line, embarrasses sentences and metaphors; before one idea has burst its shell another is hatched and clamours for inclusion.'[2]

The more recent reports on their work are in much the same

vein. On the question of dramatic workmanship generally Miss Ellis-Fermor repeats Coleridge's charge: Beaumont and Fletcher sacrifice everything to situation and immediate effect.[3] Lamb's criticism of their verse has been made again, in other words, by Mr. T. S. Eliot: imagery in the Beaumont and Fletcher verse amounts merely to dead flowers of speech planted in sand.[4] Neither as dramatists nor as poets do they seem to have the roots that clutch. Yet at the beginning of this century Shakespeare's last plays were commonly regarded as having been strongly influenced by Beaumont and Fletcher.[5] And at any time after the death of James I (Fletcher too died in 1625) something like the following comparisons would be made by the polite and instructed reader:

When Jonson, Shakespeare, and thyself did sit,
And sway'd in the triumvirate of Wit,
Yet what from Jonson's oil and sweat did flow,
Or what more easy Nature did bestow
On Shakespeare's gentler muse, in thee full grown
Their graces both appear; yet so, that none
Can say, here Nature ends and Art begins;
But mixt, like th' elements, and born like twins.[6]

Denham need carry no authority, but he is a reminder of the Caroline rating which, as a phenomenon of taste and choice, calls for understanding. There was a time when Beaumont and Fletcher seemed the universal geniuses, combining qualities which avoided on the one hand Jonson's laboured calculation of effect and on the other Shakespeare's merely random happiness:

Manners and scenes may alter, but not you;
For yours are not mere humours, gilded strains;
The fashion lost, your massy sense remains.[7]

The judgment is no doubt a mental aberration. But it was broadspread in the seventeenth century, typical of a class and a time.

I propose now to look at the position Beaumont and Fletcher occupied in their contemporary world; then, to examine what they actually did in one of their serious plays; finally, bearing in mind their present-day neglect, when practically all the other Jacobeans have had their vogue, to hazard a fresh placing of their work from the point of view of a modern observer.

I

The social positioning of Beaumont and Fletcher has often been noticed. So has the timing of their appearance. The provenance of what they put into their plays has also been commented on. What is most lacking, in their case, would seem to be that which is most needed—the linking of these things significantly, so as to make possible the right groupings and the appropriate comparisons.

Professor A. Harbage has pointed to their special position among dramatists of their time:

'In the reign of James a greater number of the writers seem to have been gentlemen by birth, but there is no change in the status of their occupation. Typical of this group was John Fletcher, well-born, and well-nurtured but *déclassé*; he lacked patrimony, his father had died in debt and in royal disfavour. Most dedicatory epistles . . . were suggestive of mendicancy, and could scarcely be written by the gentle according to the strictures of the day. The one true exception to our rule is Francis Beaumont, his father a judge in a family still prospering. But Francis was a younger son. . . .' [8]

The best sketch of Bishop Fletcher and son (Harrington only portrays the father) is given by Bishop Goodman, that anxious whitener of sepulchres wherever possible:

'Doctor Fletcher, dean of Peterborough, he was made almoner and Bishop of Bristol . . . he was afterwards preferred to London; and there he married my Lady Baker, a very handsome, beautiful woman. . . . Here many libels were made against him: I remember part of one of them:

We will divide the name of Fletcher;
He, my Lord F.; and she, my Lady Letcher.

I think he had a check from the Queen, and died for sorrow. His son was a poet to a playhouse.'[9]

Bishop Goodman's professional charity was apt to fail when confronted with failure. He obviously regarded the son's career as a fitting appendage to the father's disgrace. Harrington is kinder to the man by including in his contempt most of the courtier-Bishop's contemporaries:

'What shall I say for him? *Non erat hoc hominis vitium sed temporis?*'[10]

The original judgment of Lamb at the head of this chapter may be more fully understood in a social than in a literary sense (though it has the literary implication too). It is important either way that Beaumont and Fletcher had a Bishop and a Judge for their fathers and not a bricklayer or a small country-tradesman. The Great House, however, was not around them, as it was around Sidney: they were, after all, an inferior sort of Sidneys. The Great House was some distance away behind them, or, as an ambition, some distance in front of them: Beaumont actually did marry well and retire from the stage; Fletcher had to be content with the playhouse and the Mermaid. These he maybe succeeded in converting into something agreeable to the court *élite*—an urban substitute for Wilton and Penshurst.

The precise social placing of Beaumont and Fletcher carried with it specific differences of endowment and interest and intention as compared with those with which the popular dramatist worked. Something more, however, must be added. Beaumont and Fletcher were inferior Sidneys of the second generation. The work done within the Great House itself is different from that work which is based on it (as 'literature') but which is actually done outside its walls by persons whose right of admittance might be a matter for conjecture, for a public that would certainly, in most cases, be excluded. The distinctions are not merely snobbish. The declension is real. In Sidney's day the Great House had been a centre of culture in its own right, independent of the Court. Sidney draws a picture of it in the opening pages of the *Arcadia*—itself a typical achievement of the Great House in literature. There Lord Kalander can comment critically and with sharp detachment on the sillinesses of King Basilius, who, in leaving his palace and shirking his responsibilities, has fallen away from the standards the Great House expected the Palace to uphold. The Great House and its literature (the *Arcadia*, *The Faerie Queene*, the Pastorals, and the petrarchan sonnet-sequences) belonged to the polite Renaissance and to something consciously European. Its works were to stand comparison with those of Greece and Rome, France and Italy: epics in prose or verse compendiously analysing love and the ideal man. Beaumont and Fletcher take over from this tradition the matter of the Arcadian and pastoral and petrarchan, together with the conscious intention of the Great House to achieve literature—the intention, as it becomes with them in fact, to make the popular drama literary. In their case, however, the declension has to be reckoned in: a twofold degeneration, what Harrington would see as *vitium hominis et temporis*.

The Jacobean phase can best be seen, as the Victorians saw it, in a sinister light. In both politics and letters the Court asserted itself disastrously, to upset a precarious balance. James's claim to the kingly prerogative was not the attempt to retain something which had been granted Elizabeth. It was a bid for something Elizabeth herself had never pretended to, and which (on the terms maintained by James) had never existed. The structure behind Elizabeth's rule had been a confederation of Great Houses. Her power was merely the exertion in a single person of the reason, the competence, the influence, and the desert upon which this confederation (ideally) based itself. In the person of James the Court usurped the place the Great House had occupied. Thereby what Greville called 'the strong middle wall' was broken. Looking at the disgusting shambles of James's dramatic entertainment for the King of Denmark, Harrington remarked that it was different 'in our Queen's days'.[11] Commenting more widely, a Lord Kalander could have noted almost item by item how James was behaving like Basilius in his dotage. This political depression of the Great House and the values it represented is paralleled in the literary field by James's taking over the Chamberlain's men and making them King's Players, and by his attaching other of the actors' companies to the Queen and the Prince. The influence of the Court seems to have vulgarized both the politics and the literature of the Great House. It coarsened the technique of government and perverted taste.

It is this that makes the timing of Beaumont and Fletcher as important as the placing. The *déclassé* son of the Bishop and the younger son of the Judge are James's unconscious agents. They are capturing the Great House literature for the courtier, writing for adherents of a Stuart king rather than for Tudor aristocrats. Their work, from one point of view, represents a snobbish vulgarization and a sectional narrowing of the great tradition.

In this Beaumont and Fletcher are not alone, nor are they unrespectable. They occupy very much the same social and literary position as Donne. Donne himself was a marginal beneficiary of the Great House tradition, who survived, depressed and now utterly dependent, to write subserviently under the conditions inaugurated by James.

Donne in his *Satyres* can claim rightly:

With God and with the Muses I conferre.[12]

Or again:

On a huge hill,
Cragged, and steep, Truth stands . . .
Keep the truth which thou hast found; men do not stand
In so ill case here, that God with his hand
Sign'd Kings blanck-charters to kill whom they hate,
Nor are they Vicars but hangmen to Fate.[13]

This has the tone and independence of Kalander and the Great House. In *The Sunne Rising* (still in the pre-Jacobean period) Donne can also write:

If her eyes have not blinded thine,
Looke, and tomorrow late, tell mee,
Whether both th' India's of spice and Myne
Be where thou left'st them, or lie here with mee.
Aske for those Kings whom thou saw'st yesterday,
And thou shalt heare, All here in one bed lay.

She is all States, and all Princes, I,
Nothing else is.
Princes doe but play us; compar'd to this,
All honor's mimique; All wealth alchimie.[14]

It is the same Donne that writes the *Satyres* and *Songs and Sonets.* In the *Satyres* he takes his stand on truth and his own independent experience, on a kind of dignity which he feels due both to God and the Muse. In *Songs and Sonets*, in spite of the different content, there is a similar tone. *The Sunne Rising* gets an immediate sanction. It has tenderness, playfulness, impatience, and pride, vigorous courage and tough reasonableness. Its components, matched with hyperbole and conceit, lie well together with each other and with the form in which they are expressed. One feels confident that the poet would put things in right order of priority. Even the final hyperbole is not a lie, or a merely poetic truth. Hyperbole will eventually become one of the main Jacobean vehicles of self-persuasion: here it is the witty stretching of plain sense in order to take in more truth:

She is all States, and all Princes, I,
Nothing else is.

—'She is all the States I care about and am a loyal member of; and I am sole ruler as well as subject in this State, complete servant and complete King. Nothing else is—is important, is as much, is so completely known.'—The 'over'-statement that is presented to a first glance as an extravagance resolves itself, on a second glance, into an interesting exploration of what is generally accepted and acceptable. The effect is carried by the rich ambiguities of 'is', itself capable of meaning everything or nothing: everything if we regard it as saying 'has real Being', nothing if we see it as needing always an extension before it can mean anything; everything and nothing as it means 'is' or 'seems'.

'Is' and 'seems' and the ambiguities playing through them set up a frame that contains what immediately follows—with its almost unnoticeable inversion of what Dr. Richards has called *vehicle* and *tenour*:

Princes doe but play us; compar'd to this,
All honor's mimique; All wealth alchimie.

—Love is both an assertion and a surrender of the will, a resolved belief and a rapture. Rule, honours, and token currency are secondary phenomena, social shadows or derivatives or a language for or an expression of the primary society which two lovers form. None of them can stand in their own right, or can be so immediately known, as love can, to be more than provisionally true. They are means not ends. Their usurpation of the central position in the world would be a perverse tyranny. They command not belief, but, at the most acquiescence; their claim over us is felt not as a rapture but as coercion. Again the hyperbole is on the surface only: the direction in which it works is towards an interesting exploration of sense.

In all this Donne is in the great tradition of Sidney. He writes as the poet above the need or the desire to sing at doors for meat, as the poet exploring truth and investigating the metaphysic of love: love not as a petrarchan convention but as the key to what conventions are about. Within ten years the tone and truth of Donne's verse change. The 'truth' he was dedicated to in the *Satyres* becomes the fabrication of the compliments he there despised. The mistresses of the *Songs and Sonets* become the patronesses of the *Verse Letters*. There the riches of 'mine' and 'India', 'America' and 'coins', become suddenly concretized to the moneys he desperately needed:

She that was best and first originall
Of all fair copies, and the generall
Steward to Fate; she whose rich eyes, and breast,
Guilt the West Indies, and perfum'd the East;
Whose having breath'd in this world, did bestow
Spice on those Isles, and bade them still smell so,
And that rich Indie which doth gold interre,
Is but as single money, coyn'd from her:
She to whom this world must itself refer,
As Suburbs, or the Microcosme of her,
Shee, shee is dead; shee's dead: when thou knowst this,
Thou knowst how lame a cripple this world is.[15]

Donne here is adding image to image rather than writing poetry; and the imagery is repetitious, commercial, mercenary. What he says, furthermore, is now felt as only poetically true. The hyperboles do not extend sense: they balance permissively on a convention or a fashion of compliment.

Beaumont and Fletcher provoke comparison with the later Donne. *Non erat hoc hominis vitium sed temporis.* They are involved in the same degeneration of a tradition, impelled by similar bread-and-butter needs. It was economic pressure that deflected Donne from the metaphor of *Songs and Sonets* to the conceits of the *Anniversaries.* It was the urge of the younger son to exploit the India of the stage, the desire of the *déclassé* to rehabilitate himself in court circles (the memory and the ambition of the Great House still working in each of them) which drove Beaumont and Fletcher to descend on the popular theatre and wrest it from its popular way to something they could approve of and make their social equals applaud. This of course makes their descent on the playhouse much more consciously a social strategy than in all likelihood it was. There is, however, the fact that two of the earliest plays they wrote were, first, a burlesque of what the popular audience approved, *The Knight of the Burning Pestle* which was not well received, and second, *The Faithful Shepherdess,* a literary pastoral of which Fletcher wrote to one of James's new baronets:

> *This play was never liked, unless by few*
> *That brought their judgments with 'em.*[16]

Compared with the tradition digested naturally into the drama of Shakespeare the Sidneian world is itself a narrow thing. It is conscious and classical and avoids contacts with what in the *Arcadia* would be called the Helots. The world of Beaumont and Fletcher is still narrower. The difference is that between Penshurst and Wilton and the Court or Blackfriars. The former were European and national at the same time. The latter became something local and sectional.

Beaumont and Fletcher's social affiliations, then, are the same as Donne's; their literary tradition goes back on one side, but on the new Jacobean terms, to the Elizabethan Great House. They operate at a time when the tradition is already degenerating; they are themselves, in fact, prime agents in the degeneration—in the adaptation of platonism and petrarchanism to an inferior end and audience. Their ambition and their strategy can be represented as being a twofold invasion. On the one hand they will capture the popular playhouse, on the other they will gate-crash court society. The Sidneian matter supplied protective colouring for the latter; their dramatic facility ensured success in the former. Their work is brilliantly opportunistic. They are quick to catch and reflect back the lights of their social and literary environment. But they are not to be regarded solely as followers of fashions and tastes. Their social significance in the early Jacobean period goes deeper. They had the power to be formers of attitudes, initiators rather than mimics. They supplied the basis of what will later develop into the Cavalier mentality. In this respect their work can be compared with that of Byron. Later people—not in literature but in actual life—play out Beaumont-and-Fletcherism in their own biographies. Kenelm Digby is one of their heroes in the flesh. The early part of Herbert of Cherbury's autobiography reads like one of their plays.

It is evasive, therefore, to regard their art as merely the creation of a 'fairy world'.[17] Their plays strike roots deep into a real world—the world of their time and of the embryonic Cavalier. Their 'unreality' for us amounts to a criticism of much more than the two dramatists concerned. It is a judgment too of the habits of mind of an actual section of a historical society—a world, in spite of its heritage of charity from the Middle Ages and of instructed reason from the Great House, soon to be confronted with the situation of dictated choice in the midst of civil conflict, a world of radical self-division and clashing absolutes: the world ready to split in every way which Beaumont and Fletcher's serious plays symbolize.

We might turn now to one of these serious plays. Our purpose will be to look for signs of consistency and method. Our leading idea will be, they are not organized, as Shakespeare's plays are, by metaphor—'a key-note which guides and controls the harmonies throughout'—but rather by that which organizes

Donne's *Anniversaries*, the hyperbole and the conceit. And it is the experience organized by hyperbole and conceit which strikes the roots that clutch Beaumont and Fletcher's time. What these roots were we shall also attempt to say.

II

The central situation in *Philaster* involves three people. Arethusa, the princess, is the only child of the King. Philaster, legitimate heir to part of the Kingdom, is in love with her. Bellario is Philaster's 'page', sent by him to Arethusa to serve as their means of communication. The events of the play are set in motion by the arrival, at the Court, of Pharamond, the Spanish prince, who comes seeking the hand of Arethusa. This touches off, first, the rebellion story: the group of courtiers led by Dion are unwilling for Philaster's legitimate claims to be put on one side, as Philaster himself is too. Secondly, Pharamond's incontinence while at the Court (the reverse side, as in *Songs and Sonets*, of the idealistic petrarchan woman-worship) leads to the calumny which will start rotating the relations between the three in the central triangle. Pharamond is discovered early in his stay with a loose waiting-woman who avoids publicity by accusing Arethusa of similar looseness with Bellario, and thus blackmails the King into silence. This lie is repeated to Philaster by Dion. Dion is intent on Philaster's leading the popular revolt and breaking with Arethusa.

A larger frame is sketchily suggested for the central happenings in the play: the King, like Henry IV, is aware of the guilty means whereby he has come to the throne and is depriving Philaster of his just inheritance. He sees his misfortunes as part of a providential punishment for his sins. Arethusa too feels that providence is at work—in her case, a providence working through romantic love for the restoration of justice.

The retention of this traditional providence supervising the working out of the plot might be significant. It is not what we think of as the typically Beaumont-and-Fletcherian. It seems rather to be a gesture in the direction of something Shakespearian. (Philaster is moved by the spirit of his 'father' as Hamlet was, and the King's guilty conscience is reminiscent of Claudius as well as Henry IV.) Though the King, Arethusa, and the courtiers more than once underline it in their speeches, it might be intended merely as a familiar colouring for the story, the better to insinuate what was essentially new. The references to providence, in any case, belong to the outer shell of the play. The inner core, wherein the novelty consists, and in which the main seriousness of the dramatists is displayed, is the platonic or petrarchan triangle of the lovers. It is the happenings here that I propose to concentrate attention on. These provide almost all the 'situations' and 'dramatic effects' to which Beaumont and Fletcher are said to sacrifice everything: coherence of character, moral integrity, artistic unity.

The basis of the emotional attitudes throughout is a prevailing disposition to wilful belief, belief as an all-or-nothing reaction, consciously directed, an absolute self-commitment. The typical Beaumont and Fletcher situations turn on the divisions that such rival absolutes bring about when the central characters find themselves between two or more of them.

In *Philaster* (as in the plays generally) one of these absolutes is the King. At one point in the play the King's absoluteness is given a satiric or comic turn. The princess Arethusa is lost in the forest and her father is commanding that she shall be found:

KING. *I do command you all, as you are subjects,*
To show her me! What! am I not your King?
If ay, then am I not to be obeyed?
DION. *Yes, if you command things possible and honest.*
KING. *Things possible and honest! Hear me, thou,*
Thou traitor, that do'st confine thy King to things
Possible and honest! show her me,
Or let me perish if I cover not
All Sicily with blood.
DION. *Indeed I cannot,*
Unless you tell me where she is. (IV. ii.)

But brute facts call the King's bluff and he is forced at length to realize his limitations:

Alas! What are we Kings!
Why do ye gods place us above the rest,
To be served, flattered, and adored, till we
Believe we hold within our hands your thunder,
And when we come to try the power we have
There's not a leaf shakes at our threatenings?
I have sinned, 'tis true, and here stand to be punished
Yet would not thus be punished: let me choose
My way, and lay it on!

DION. *He articles with the gods. Would somebody would draw bonds for the performance of covenants betwixt them.* (IV. ii.)

We have said that this passage is comic or satiric. To be so definitive is maybe over-precipitate. There seems, rather, to be a mixture, or a confusion, or a wavering between intentions in its treatment. Clearly, however, the scene cannot be claimed for full seriousness. The King is not Lear, and Dion is neither Kent nor the Fool. The significant thing is the way the characters fling themselves into disparate roles, adopting one extreme stance after another with all-or-nothing wilfulness. The roles have nothing in common except the wilfulness behind them. The King will be absolute King, the King will be patient sinner suffering the strokes of the gods. Dion (who could have been made a Lord Kalander or a Kent) remains the debunking commentator on both, not disinterested but uninterested in what he says. Neither Dion nor the King seem to have anything in common, not even common humanity, nor the common relationship of King and subject. Instead, they both seem to be embodiments, as it were, of the attitudes they voice—attitudes, again, that the romantics would accuse of having no organic interconnection, and between which transition can only be made by violent self-galvanizations of the will.

If the scene itself is not to be taken seriously, the frequent occurrence of such scenes in the plays must be. It is profoundly symptomatic of Beaumont. Though he is not being clearly satirical or comic, and while the total effect is too confused for full artistic seriousness, there is no doubt that seriousness is intended. The point is that Beaumont's mind works like the minds of his characters, and he is involved in quandaries similar to theirs. He lacks the supporting strength of an independent position from which to see with detachment what he is writing about. Sidney had this strength and support through membership of the Great House: his portrait of Basilius, therefore, is steady and unequivocal. Jonson and Shakespeare had the strength and independence of yet another tradition which enabled them to comment on Kingship, in plays like *Sejanus* or *King Lear*, with equal unmistakeability. Beaumont has no steady ground to stand on. His attitude to the King, therefore (to take the single example of this scene) inevitably wavers. Beaumont himself is surrounded by the clamorous absolutes which have to be chosen among and which it is nonsense to choose among. But choice is dictated for him. He is himself deeply engaged in the attitudes he is writing about, and in the attitude of mind which makes 'attitudes' important. He is responding deeply to something in his environment. He is a part of his contemporary situation in a pejorative sense.

There is also the fact of Beaumont's adolescence which is relevant here. His concern with attitudes and choice is adolescent—the adolescent as the parvenu to the adult world who brings with him all the virgin will to be convinced, but who has not yet had the time to acquire the wisdom that would illuminate what he is choosing and bring relevant order to his convictions. Beaumont and Fletcher's work indicates the collapse of a culture, an adult scheme is being broken up and replaced by adolescent intensities. It is this which makes the Caroline rating of their work, as compared with that of Jonson and Shakespeare, such a bad augury.

The scene with Dion and the King is about as bad as Beaumont and Fletcher can be. It does, however, reveal the kind of forces among which even their good scenes are set, and the kind of 'situation' we have to deal with in reading them. These 'situations' have much to do with 'psychology', but little to do with the naturalism of consistent character-portrayal. The psychology is that of a blind compulsion to be certain and to be convinced. It is the psychology, too, of a time when action was demanded on the basis of the conviction entertained; and when loyalties were being solicited by widely different authorities.

Kingship is only one of the absolutes in the general Beaumont and Fletcher environment. They are not interested in assessment of any of the absolutes separately, and are weakest when they pretend to be. Their best work is done where their main interest lies—in the conflict of the absolutes and the contortions it imposes on human nature.

In Act I, Scene i, this typical inner setting is swiftly arranged. Philaster comes into the Presence to challenge Pharamond's right to replace him as heir to the throne. He begins by making his obeisances to the King:

Right noble sir, as low as my obedience,
And with a heart as loyal as my knee
I beg your favour.

The King gives him permission, within the bounds proper to a subject, to say what he will. Philaster then immediately turns on Pharamond, and threatens him with hyperbolical rebellion if ever he should take the throne. The King intervenes to check him; Philaster's defiance collapses:

I am dead, sir; you're my fate. It was not I
Said I was wronged.

The King thinks Philaster must be possessed. Philaster rejoins that he is possessed—and with his father's spirit:

It's here, O King,
A dangerous spirit! now he tells me, King,
I was a King's heir, bids me be a King,
And whispers to me, these are all my subjects . . .
But I'll suppress him; he's a factious spirit,
And will undo me. Noble sir, your hand;
I am your servant.
KING. *Away! I do not like this:*
I'll make you tamer, or I'll dispossess you
Both of your life and spirit. For this time
I pardon your wild speech, without so much
As your imprisonment.

There is no suggestion of satire here. The King is one of the absolutes Philaster recognizes. The demands of justice (the 'spirit' of his father) are another. But there is no moral conflict in Philaster. He can live absolutely in either the one loyalty or the other. It is a law of the Beaumont world that absolute committal removes the need for moral deliberation, and supervenes on conflict by suppression of one of the warring terms. The courtiers, Philaster's friends, for example, are bent on revolt:

shrink not, worthy sir,
But add your father to you; in whose name
We'll waken all the gods, and conjure up
The rods of vengeance, the abused people,
Who, like raging torrents . . .

But Philaster does not so much as feel the pressure of their rhetoric:

Friends, no more;
Our ears may be corrupted; 'tis an age
We dare not trust our wills to.

The audience is left, at the end of this first scene, with an exciting sense of an either-or world, and of a hero who will be all-or-nothing whichever way he is thrown: for it is obvious he won't (in the normal sense of the word) decide. There is this, and a further sense besides—something that comes through in Philaster's words last quoted: the sense that this is not only literary entertainment, but literature aware of itself as a symptom rather than a reflection of the dangerous reality surrounding it—aware of a world that cannot be trusted, and in which the mind is forced back upon itself to make a world of its own, by belief, or resolve, or art:

'tis an age
We dare not give our wills to.

The other sphere in which the absolutes manifest themselves for the Beaumont hero we are introduced to in the scene immediately following. Arethusa sends for Philaster. Up to now neither he nor the audience have had any inkling of what is to take place. But Arethusa is in love with Philaster. The scene is a minor example of the stunts with situation which characterize all the Beaumont and Fletcher plays: the subject cannot woo the princess, so the princess will declare her love to the subject. More than this, it is an interesting example of Beaumont's technique exerting itself on a more serious level. Its congruency with what has gone before it and with what will follow after helps to credibilize the incredibles later to be handled.

Arethusa's inversion of propriety is justified by invoking the overruling power of the gods. She is driven by forces larger than human:

'tis the gods,
The gods that make me so; and, sure, our love
Will be the nobler and the better blest,
In that the secret justice of the gods
Is mingled with it. (I. ii.)

But this divine sanction is in fact supererogatory: love itself is an absolute for the Beaumont and Fletcher lovers.

Secondly, there is the teasing way in which the proposal is made. Philaster assumes (the audience is already aware of what is in Arethusa's mind) that a declaration of love is the last thing that will be made in the interview. And Arethusa's first words seem to bear out his fears. Why, she asks, has he laid scandal on her in a public place, and called the great part of her dowry in question? Philaster's reply is similar to his original reaction to the King:

Madam, this truth which I shall speak will be
Foolish; but for your fair and virtuous self,
I could afford myself to have no right
To anything you wished.

Notwithstanding, Philaster confesses he is loath to give

His right unto a sceptre and a crown
To save a lady's longing.

He is still unaware that Arethusa is in love with him. Arethusa then says she must have both kingdoms, and even more. Philaster must turn away his face while she tells him the full length of her demands. At this Philaster flies into heroics:

I can endure it. Turn away my face!
I never yet saw enemy that looked
So dreadfully but that I thought myself
So great a basilisk as he; or spake
So horribly but that I thought my tongue
Bore thunder underneath, as much as his;
Nor beast that I could turn from: shall I then
Begin to fear sweet sounds? a lady's voice
Whom I do love? Say, you would have my life;
Why, I will give it you; for 'tis to me
A thing so loathed, and unto you that ask
Of so poor use, that I will make no price:
If you entreat I will unmovedly hear.

This is wit according to Dr. Johnson's formula: contrary ideas yoked together by violence. It is witty in that what the audience knows is love on Arethusa's part, Philaster takes to be hate; what he thinks is a demand about to be made on him the audience knows is an offer about to be made to him. Philaster's misapprehension has been successfully raised at this point to hyperbolical proportions. And in one and the same speech we see his heroism and his helplessness, his worth and his sense of worthlessness asserted.

But a measure of depth and seriousness can be recognized in the admittedly adolescent mood in which the hero and the scene are conceived. The part somehow seems to become greater than the whole, the contortions of the hero more important than the forces that produce them. The fact that Philaster is labouring under a misapprehension does not make for complacency in the spectator; and the heroics—on a fair reading—are not received as ridiculous. From this point of view the scene works like a joke that has been pushed too far: except that it never has been a joke. Arethusa's apparently teasing lack of straightforwardness is in keeping with her situation. She must be assured that Philaster would in any case give himself utterly before she can offer herself utterly to him. The point is in that 'utterly'—the adolescent all-or-nothing terms in which the commitments are conceived.

The scene in any case works two ways. There is the joke that it will all have a happy ending. There is also the sense, fatal to our taking the joke at its face value, that happiness as a conclusion to what the scene reveals is an irrelevance. Philaster's heroic and pathetic self-contortion, his insistent readiness to give himself utterly (misapprehension or no) to love or death, are part of a tragi-comedy that cannot really be happy.

There is a final aspect of the Beaumont and Fletcher manner which this scene illustrates, a factor which still further assists belief in Philaster's reactions later. This is the monadic self-enclosure of the characters—part of the petrarchan convention of love, or a part of the native adolescence of Beaumont's mind. The lover can be completely insulated within his love, regardless of the beloved. Love is not necessarily a mutual contract, it can be a private direction of the will, like prayer; or a service, like virtue, that justifies itself by being its own reward. This quality comes out in the scene when Arethusa has finally confessed her love to Philaster, and he replies:

Madam, you are too full of noble thoughts
To lay a train for this contemned life,
Which you may have for asking: to suspect
Were base, where I deserve no ill. Love you!
By all my hopes, I do, above my life!
But how this passion should proceed from you
So violently, would amaze a man
That would be jealous.

The world of Beaumont is a violent, extreme, arbitrary, sudden, and wilful thing, ready at any moment to be inverted, or to swing from one contrary to another. We have seen how the external plot is arranged so that opposite pulls can be exerted at any minute on the main characters, and how—with Philaster in the first scene—the loyalty of the subject is absolute but never complete, since it can only be maintained by an actively willed suppression of the disloyalty he also shares in. Here, the opposites are introjected into the heart of what might seem the only single certainty and purity the Beaumont lovers can find. Love itself, in the moment of its most open and utter declaration, is recognized to be an incalculable force, ambivalently sinister in its possibilities: binding and yet disruptive:

> *how this passion should proceed from you*
> *So violently, would amaze a man*
> *That would be jealous.*

Philaster sees the chaste and hitherto inaccessible model of womanhood suddenly proposing to him. He is overwhelmed, but of course ready to accept. In the midst of his confusion he is able to note the possible ambiguity of Arethusa's behaviour for an interpreter that '*would* be jealous'. His 'amazement' is another stroke of wit, and an oddly serious one. He loved Arethusa apart from any hope of reciprocation: in spite of her impossibility and almost because of it. (The 'psychology' is the same here as in Marvell's poem.) Now that the Impossible She is so possible, the possibility might itself argue an imperfection. Philaster will love her, of course, on the new terms still. But these will require suppression of the interpretation just glimpsed. A fresh tension is thereby introduced. And when Arethusa is calumniated, as she is soon to be, the scales will tilt again, the disruption will begin, and inverted petrarchanism show itself in near-obscenity and disgust of life. The conception in this scene prepares us to accept Philaster's subsequent misbelief of Arethusa.

It is a scene well contrived within the limits of the initial sonneteerish postulates. It might even be claimed to carry more conviction then Leontes' jealousy, or the somersault of Posthumus; though, it must be added, Shakespeare was not really interested in the postulates Beaumont adopted, and does not seem to have bothered overmuch with the mechanics appropriate to them.

Act II springs the trap which has been prepared for Philaster's love. Arethusa is accused of intimacy with Bellario, the Viola-like page Philaster sent her. (In justice to Beaumont's workmanship it might be pointed out that again we have been prepared for the sort of thing the calumniators report: In Act II, Scene iv, misconduct with pages is represented as almost habitual in court circles.) Act III is devoted to Philaster's reception of the report, his interview with Bellario (who is in love with him) and his encounter with Arethusa herself.

Close analysis of this act (a most effective one) would not carry insight into Beaumont's technique much further. There is no increment of growing wisdom in the situation as it develops. Beaumont's plays, in fact, have no developing revelations, crowded as they are with surprises and fresh turns. For all the increasing violence and cleverness of their movement they seem to get nowhere. The return is always to the original starting-point: the petrarchan nexus, the adolescent all-or-nothingness, the willed and rigid stance on one set of assumptions maintained by the resolved suppression of another, the sense of an arbitrary outer world and a dissociated inner one, of rifts that cannot be bridged but must be desperately overleapt, the mêlée of absolute claims and exaggerated postures—an agony of self-scision based on misapprehension and brought back (by the external contrivances of the plot) to a 'happy' conclusion: a curious sense, typical of decadence, of something at once more primitive and more sophisticated than the normal.

But while it does not further insight into the essential Beaumont situation Act III is a good example of what we have called the 'extended conceit'. This is particularly true of the scene between Philaster and Bellario.

Philaster has just received his friend Dion's account of Arethusa's scandalous behaviour. He is soliloquising on the theme 'What the eye doesn't see'; how, for animals, nothing is but what is seen; but for man, nothing is (at times) but what is not:

O that like beasts we could not grieve ourselves
With what we see not! Bulls and rams will fight
To keep their females, standing in their sight:
But take 'em from them and you take at once
Their spleens away; and they will fall again
Unto their pastures; growing fresh and fat;
And taste the waters of the springs as sweet
As 'twas before, finding no start in sleep;
But miserable man—— (III. i.)

—and at this point Bellario enters. The rest of the speech (it can be imagined well enough) will be demonstrated in action on the stage rather than compressed into metaphor. Philaster is amazed that Bellario, the monster of lust and ingratitude, should still look outwardly the same as he has always done:

> *See, see, you gods,*
> *He walks still; and the face you let him wear*
> *When he was innocent is still the same,*
> *Not blasted! Is this justice? do you mean*
> *To intrap mortality, that you allow*
> *Treason so smooth a brow? I cannot now*
> *Think he is guilty.*

The speech carries on the ruminations of the soliloquy. It works too a kind of trick with intellectual mirrors, animating all the confusions between 'is' and 'seems' in which mortality can so easily entrap itself, precipitating Philaster into the midst of these confusions, where he finds himself choosing again—hurling himself on the desperate other side of the gulf he has opened out before himself: he cannot now think Bellario is guilty. The volte-face is well executed, and restores both sides of Philaster's self-division to equal status; the prerequisite for Beaumont's strongest occasions.

The remainder of the scene is constructed wittily along similar lines. Beaumont exploits fully the device of double-consciousness (or even double-talk) which is expressive of something central in his conception. The divided man confronts the integral, and mistakes it. Bellario is really innocent. Philaster thinks instead he is the consummate actor of innocence. Philaster will therefore act the part to compete with this, and hoist the engineer with his own petard. The mirror effects begin to multiply.

Philaster inquires how Bellario has been treated while with Arethusa:

> *Tell me, my boy, how doth the princess use thee?*
> *For I shall guess her love to me by that.*

Bellario gives his innocent account of all Arethusa's favours. Philaster is caught by the reviving shock of his love and disgust. He recovers and presses Bellario harder. We are shown the familiar reverse side of petrarchan idealism. The catastrophic overthrow of his love (only possible by reason of his 'noble' mind and the 'virtue' it would espouse) releases an unmanageable and compulsive evil within him. Philaster is as much bound now to the most squalid prurience as he was formerly to the chastest adoration. And the agent of his overthrow, whom he would make the pander to his itch for obscenities, is the innocent 'page' he regards as his greatest friend, and who (beneath it all) is really a girl faithfully in love with him—and thus doubly incapable of disloyalty. It is easy to see what the generation which produced the metaphysicals saw in such scenes as this. It is the 'conceit' perfectly stage-managed, without the overt imagery of conceit:

PHIL. *She kisses thee?*
BEL. *Not so, my lord.*
PHIL. *Come, come, I know she does.*
BEL. *No, by my life.*
PHIL. *Why then she does not love me. Come, she does:*
I bade her do it; I charged her by all charms
Of love between us, by the hope of peace
We should enjoy, to yield thee all delights
Naked as to her bed; I took her oath
Thou should'st enjoy her. Tell me, gentle boy,
Is she not parallelless? is not her breath
Sweet as Arabian winds when fruits are ripe?
Are not her breasts two liquid ivory balls?
Is she not all a lasting mine of joy?
BEL. *Ay, now I see why my disturbed thoughts*
Were so perplexed: when first I went to her
My heart held augury. You are abused;
Some villain hath abused you: I do see
Whereto you tend. Fall rocks upon his head
That put this to you! 'tis some subtle train
To bring that noble frame of yours to nought.
PHIL. *Thou think'st I will be angry with thee. Come,*
Thou shalt know all my drift; I hate her more
Than I love happiness, and placed thee there

To pry with narrow eyes into her deeds.
Hast thou discovered? is she fallen to lust,
As I would wish her? Speak some comfort to me.
BEL. *My lord, you did mistake the boy you sent:*
Had she the lust of sparrows or of goats,
Had she a sin that way, hid from the world,
Beyond the name of lust, I would not aid
Her base desires: but what I came to know
As servant to her, I would not reveal,
To make my life last ages.

The code of Honour sets a final and inescapable trap for its observers. Absolute loyalty forbids any telling of tales, even when a friend or a lover commands. Honour itself can thus ally with deception. Philaster has to proceed to threats:

oh, my heart!
This is a salve worse than the main disease.
Tell me thy thoughts; for I will know the least
(Draws his sword)
That dwells within thee, or rip thy heart
To know it: I will see thy thoughts as plain
As I do now thy face.

At the climax of his rage he returns to the thought with which he began on first seeing Bellario.

The rest of the scene solves the problem of Philaster's transition from threatening Bellario's life to sending him away still loved but still thought to be the deceiver. The moves are worked with the same skill, but still continuing within the narrow and violent compass of the petrarchan and adolescent postulates. The note on which Philaster ends is the second return to the dilemma of what things are and what they seem. This time the resolution seems magnanimous:

Rise, Bellario:
Thy protestations are so deep, and thou
Dost look so truly when thou utter'st them,
That, though I know them false as were my hopes,
I cannot urge thee further. But thou wert

To blame to injure me, for I must love
Thy honest looks, and take no revenge upon
Thy tender youth: a love from me to thee
Is firm, whate'er thou dost . . .
. . . But, good boy,
Let me not see thee more: something is done
That will distract me, that will make me mad
If I behold thee.

The mood, however, is not one of firm resolve. It is rather the passing stability of exhaustion in the midst of fever. All the items of Philaster's self-division are still present. Only the informing energies that usually stir them to conflict are absent. The verse moves to the rhythm of a relaxed exhaustion. In the lull of the violent fit Philaster is at length able to hold together all the opposites. He can call up again the absolute of his affection for the page, and recognizes too that it will be overthrown at any moment by 'distraction'. Occasions like this show how firmly Beaumont has hold on what he is doing, and how consistent is his conception.

What is it that Beaumont is doing? To analyse the serious scenes that ensue would tell us little more than is already apparent from those examined so far. Philaster sees Arethusa, in a subdued mood he confesses himself her slave, her

creature, made again from what it was
And newly-spirited. (III. ii.)

Then, stirred again, he reviles both himself and her. He echoes Donne's *A Lecture upon a Shadow:*

all the good you have is but a shadow,
I' the morning with you, and at night behind you.

He goes off into the forest which provides a fitting back-drop for the Beaumont and Fletcher worlds, both inner and outer. Here the court hunts, and court ladies disappear into convenient brakes. Here the normal countryman can comment on his betters in much the same vein as Harrington commented on the hunting parties of James and the King of Denmark. Here a brute creation seems to pursue the rational.[18] Lovers wound themselves and wound each other, and seek death in the pastoral environment they otherwise long for as the asylum from their conflicts and confusions. At times the Beaumont vision strikes through the verse. There is resonance, for example, in Arethusa's cry at the end of Act III, Scene ii, when Philaster has left her and she is called to join her father's hunting:

I am in tune to hunt!
Diana, if thou canst rage with a maid
As with a man, let me discover thee
Bathing, and turn me to a fearful hind,
That I may die pursued by cruel hounds,
And have my story written in my wounds.

The forest, above all, is where the heroes and heroines get lost, with the lostness that is recurrent in Beaumont:

Where am I now? Feet, find me out a way,
Without the counsel of my troubled head:
I'll follow you boldly about these woods,
O'er mountains, through brambles, pits, and floods,
Heaven, I hope, will ease me: I am sick. (IV. iii.)

And in the same forest where all seems confused, the feet of the plot somehow find a way, and bring everything to a happy ending. The fourth act is as clever in its transitions from the climaxes of the third as it is in its preparation for the surprises and dénouement of the fifth.

III

We have concentrated our commentary on the petrarchan part of the play, and on only a part of that. There is much else in Beaumont and Fletcher that has received more attention. It is, however, the treatment of the love-triangle which, it seems to me, belongs particularly to their seriousness both as conscious analysts and unconscious symptoms of a particular human plight. The dramatists (or Beaumont alone, if he was solely responsible) attain in their handling of the petrarchan a personal inflection which is both distinctive and distinguished. The main roots that clutch in their work strike down through this into the heart of their time.

The petrarchan matter indicates their derivation. They are in the tradition which began with the Great House, the source of the Arcadian, Heroic, and Pastoral, as well as of the sonnet sequences, the literature of the Elizabethan *élite*. Their derivation is important from the social as well as from the literary point of view. Or rather, the literary importance does not exist apart from the social. That both Shakespeare and Beaumont and Fletcher went to the same Arcadian and Romance sources at about the same time means two things, not one. Different interests were involved, and different intentions, and these were in part the result of differences in their respective social placings. On a superficial glance alone, it is obvious that Beaumont and Fletcher, as 'inferior Sidneys', the shabby genteel of the Great House, cannot usefully be compared with Shakespeare until the important prior distinctions between the two have first been made. Their prime affiliations are not with the tradition in which Shakespeare wrote but with the tradition—however degenerate—of the Sidneians and the metaphysicals.

A close examination of *Philaster* only brings out more clearly the difference in content and conception between their romances and those of Shakespeare's last period. On their own ground Shakespeare could not compete with them. Nor would he, one can suppose, have been minded to. The intensely narrowed world in which they are at home is one which Shakespeare's maturity cannot be conceived as entering. At the same time it is evident that Beaumont and Fletcher could have learnt nothing to their essential purposes from Shakespeare's last plays. Their own romances are a genre peculiar to themselves, in spite of the surface lights from *Antony*, *Lear*, *Othello*, *Hamlet*, and possibly *Troilus*, which they reflect. If it is a case of influence one on another it would seem likely that the Victorians were right, and that Shakespeare was the debtor. Paradoxically, in a case like this it is easier to imagine the greater taking a cue from the lesser—and then going off on its own. *The Winter's Tale* and *Cymbeline* do resemble the Beaumont romances. Structural resemblance we should not expect, but resemblance in the incidentals and externals there certainly is. However, Shakespeare's last plays, internally, belong to the body of his own writing, and through that to the tradition in which they were produced. Their framework is the large metaphor his work had established for him before Beaumont and Fletcher began to write.

Beaumont and Fletcher are dramatic opportunists. *Philaster*, besides its petrarchan core, has quick and successful utilizations of the large themes of the maturer drama; the theme of rebellion, of the guilty King on the throne, the theme of the King John who turns to a Falconbridge in time of trouble. (Philaster gathers up the roles of Falconbridge, Hal, and Hamlet as ancillary to his main role of lover-hero.) But it is the petrarchan core which is important for the final assessment of the two dramatists.

We have said that it is by reason of the petrarchan matter, as they treat it, that their work strikes roots into their time. Petrarchanism is an important aspect of the Renaissance. It held out the opportunity to concentrate on a territory sealed off from the other realities, social, ethical, or religious. It hinted seductively that a social code, the basis of morality, the effects of religious discipline, could all be found in the ceremonial cult of Stella or Astrea. Ideal love would be in itself a liberal education. It would be open, also, only to such as had the leisure and the facilities of the Great House around them. Petrarchanism was both insulated and aristocratic. In the case of Beaumont the insulation works to make the large traditional themes marginal, reducing them to convenient plot-ingredients.

The roots of petrarchanism, however, strike deeper than this, particularly in the Beaumont and Fletcherian drama. Its real importance there is that the central love-triangle, conflict and self-contortion in the setting of the absolutes, presented a small-scale model and a disguise for the larger situations of real life: situations of dictated choice, of self-commitment, of wilful belief that looks like headstrong denial—situations suited to the extremities of the emotional partisan. (The reign of James brought the question of partisanship to the forefront in almost every sphere.) In the person of Philaster the embryonic Cavalier could live through in pantomime what he would later have to live through in fact except that the terms would be changed. The Beaumont hero feels himself already 'fated'. He is cut off from the social past and the neighbourly present and his future includes only death. He is absolved from the need to exert rational control, and incapable of compromise. He is self-enclosed in the splintering world of the contending absolutes, and all the violence of activity these call out can only end in self-destruction. The fated lover-hero of the Beaumont drama is one of the great premonitory symbols of the seventeenth century.

Thus plays like *Philaster* are not merely passively addressed to the tastes of their audience. They play an active role. They catch at the half-felt or the unconscious and give it expression. Beaumont and Fletcher do not cater superficially, they shape for their audience the attitudes and postures the audience is not wholly aware yet that they will need. On a most cursory view, of course, as we have tried to show, Beaumont and Fletcher clearly aimed at a two-level appeal. Their plays could easily compete with the popular theatre in dramatic stir and skill; they had something to offer, too, to the aristocrat whose poetic reading was Donne, whose private pastime was the Sonnet, and whose connoisseurship was reserved for 'wit'.

The main poetic feature of Beaumont and Fletcher is their adaptation to the stage of the sonneteer's material and the sonneteer's 'conceit'. The primary affiliation of their drama is with the Sidneians and the metaphysicals. That this should have been overlooked may be a result of the recent concentration, in criticism, on the *imagery* of poetry: the fashion for what Dr. I. A. Richards has called 'metaphor-hunting'. Clearly, poetry is not to be limited to the devising of *imagery* narrowly conceived. Our indifference to the poetry of Sidney, Spenser, and Jonson, with its accompanying exaltation of Donne, Herbert, and Marvell, may eventually be recognized as a by-product of Mr. T. S. Eliot's personal pamphleteering for what—even in him—was to be merely a chapter in his own poetic development. In any case, the absence of 'verbal texture' in Beaumont and Fletcher's verse is not decisive. Their words are stretched in the frame of their situations, and it is the frame which gives them the manifoldness of 'wit'. Their achievement was to make dramatic situation perform the work of metaphysical conceit.

A play like *Philaster*, we have said, further, leaves one with a sense of something at once more sophisticated and more primitive than the normal, of something we associate with decadence. Each of the operative words here can bear fuller expansion.

The world they construct is a product of sophistication. Sophistication implies immediate viability within a restricted circle; a degree of knowledgeability in the extreme, which yet never reaches as far as wisdom; a specialness of insight and an extreme localization of field; an intensity that fails to bring breadth of view, and which breadth of view would render impossible. Beaumont's work has this sophistication. It comes, I have argued, from his concentration on the petrarchan matter, with interests even more circumscribed than those of Sidney. And even Sidney's tradition was narrower, less mixed, and less ancient than that of Shakespeare. It would be wrong, however, to think of Beaumont and Fletcher as deliberately constructing a 'fairy world'. Their artefact is more sinister and more serious than that. It is more like the *Anniversaries* than Hans Anderson.

The world into which Beaumont and Fletcher fit, as the Victorians used to insist, however clumsily and vaguely, is the world of James I and fermenting civil war. They can be regarded from one point of view as unconsciously fighting a rearguard action on behalf of the Court, compensating with advances in Blackfriars for the retreats in Westminster. The importance of Philaster is that he foreshadows figures in real life: figures of the same class and temper as Kenelm Digby, who married, *ad maiorem gloriam amoris*, an alleged courtesan.

In history as in the Beaumont drama the setting for the main actors was one in which all-or-nothing, and either-or, were continually presented as the alternatives for choice. The absolutes of Justice for the subject, Loyalty to the King, Faith in God, Obedience to Church Discipline—a medley of incompatible demands surrounded the individual. Behaviour could no longer be regulated by agreed social habits, or by decent mutualizations of differences as between souls naturally Christian. The outer world and the inner world were beginning to exhibit the phenomena of fissure. In such a situation belief does tend to become wilful and hyperbolical, resting on suppressions and assertions combined. The Philaster hero focusses all this, and becomes the kind of Byron-model for his generation. In him the conflicts, self-divisions and desperate stands, the distraction and the longing for certainty, the bewildered lostness and the violence which will destroy what it loves and finally turn on itself—pathetically and comically jumbled, all the agonies and irresponsibilities meet.

And yet Lord Falkland can be seen as part of Beaumont's world, as well as Kenelm Digby. He too was one who did not want civil war, and yet was confronted with it. He did not wish to take sides, yet when all were fighting he must fight too, and only one side could be taken. And the story goes that on the eve of Newbury he prepared himself as if for his own burial, went out to battle in clean linen, was lost at the head of his cavalry among the opposing ranks, and was discovered next day dead on the field—the kind of suicide without self-slaughter a Philaster would have willed for himself, or Arethusa wished:

I am in tune to hunt!
Diana . . . let me discover thee
Bathing, and turn me to a fearful hind,
That I may die pursued by cruel hounds,
And have my story written in my wounds.

The primitive quality in the play is what we should expect from a decaying or collapsing culture. It is congruent, too, with what we have called the adolescent in Beaumont's conception. Both the primitive and the adolescent indicate a reversion to the premature imposed on a civilization by the new and unmanageable developments taking place inside it. Beaumont was only twenty-four when *Philaster* was written. It is not likely that he should have become maturer as he got older. His adolescence lent itself to the requirements of the time more than Jonson's detached satire could do, or Shakespeare's socially unuseable inclusiveness of comprehension. What we call the modern world was about to launch on a phase when the adolescent and the wilful had special survival value. Since Beaumont's day our society has become increasingly partisan, increasingly juvenile in its wilfulness and its unwisdom. Beaumont and Fletcher are, in an unfortunate sense, the first of the moderns. Their counterpart in the nineteenth century, we suggested, was Byron. A contemporary parallel to their work might be that of Graham Greene. The decadence they reflect has been a condition permanent since their time, and, if anything, apt to be aggravated.

CHAPTER SEVEN

The Maid's Tragedy

Without the hollow extravagance of Beaumont and Fletcher's ultra-royalism, how carefully does Shakespeare acknowledge and reverence the eternal distinction between the mere individual, and the symbolic or representative, on which all genial law, no less than patriotism, depends.

S. T. COLERIDGE, *Lectures on Shakespeare.* (Bohn Edn.), p. 260

Shakespeare gives the permanent politics of human nature, and the only predilection which appears shows itself in his contempt of mobs and the populacy. Massinger is a decided Whig;—Beaumont and Fletcher high-flying, passive-obedience Tories.

Ibid., p. 437

Coleridge was quite certain that Beaumont and Fletcher were 'servile *jure divino* royalists'. J. St. Loe Strachey, introducing the Mermaid Edition of their plays in 1887, was equally sure that such a charge was nonsense: all the evidence of *The Maid's Tragedy* is against such a generalization. There the vicious king meets his death at the hands of the woman he has seduced, and the killing is attended 'with every detail of indignity'. Yet, in a general way, as has been argued in the last chapter, Coleridge was right. Beaumont and Fletcher belong with the royalist courtiers, and fostered the outlook later to be adopted broadly by them. Both sides of the paradox have been stated recently by the late Tucker Brooke:

'Hardly anything about the Beaumont-Fletcher-Massinger pieces is more remarkable than the abnormally low quality of the kings who display themselves in this literature written of, by, and for cavaliers.'[1]

The kings in the main are 'likely to be bumptious, lecherous, and strangely unintelligent'. Professor Tucker Brooke, comparing the Elizabethan Heywood with the Jacobeans, goes on to comment:

'One could hardly wish a clearer measure of the difference between the Red Bull Playhouse and the Blackfriars, or between the Elizabethan and the Jacobean spirit. Nor could one want a better instance of the speed and completeness with which the social mode and *mores* can transform themselves, or of the accuracy with which the stage's camera eye records such things.'[2]

Furthermore, popular as Beaumont and Fletcher were after the Restoration, *The Maid's Tragedy* was one of their plays deliberately kept off the stage in deference to Charles II's wishes. It dealt too openly with the theme of 'Killing the King'. Of this dangerous practice Dryden wrote:

'the seeds were sown in the time of Queen Elizabeth, the bloody harvest ripened in the reign of Charles the Martyr.'[3]

The confusion in the discussion of Beaumont and Fletcher and their attitude to kings has come, I think, from the literary equivalent of what in philosophy Whitehead has called 'the fallacy of misplaced concreteness': the habit of abstracting a part and then ascribing to it the sort of reality that can only be assumed for the whole. More simply, it is the fallacy of treating literature as propaganda.

There can be little doubt that Beaumont and Fletcher, broadly speaking, were 'royalist'. There is no doubt that the King in *The Maid's Tragedy* is vicious and is murdered, or that Arbaces in *A King and No King* is vainglorious and strangely unintelligent. The confusion arises when either the 'passive obedience' or the 'king-killing' is treated in isolation.

Philaster, as we have seen, emphatically underlines the King's divine right. But the king was only one of the absolutes. There were in addition two others: the absolute of petrarchan love, and the absolute of Honour. Beaumont's range is narrow almost to the point of obsession, both in his themes and in his choice of characters to carry the themes. *The Maid's Tragedy* uses the same type-characters as *Philaster*, and restricts itself in the main to manipulating the same themes. And in *The Maid's Tragedy* as in *Philaster* Beaumont's interest is in the conflicts imposed on the central characters by the rival absolutes. This imparts to his plays a peculiar theatrical integrity. He is not interested in 'character', nor is he interested in the final weighing of the large themes he uses. He is interested in *situations*—in those situations of conflict which rival loyalties bring along with them, which circumstances alone can manœuvre into existence, and which choices can only perpetuate or aggravate. Such a conception needs *plotting*, it needs just those gifts which Beaumont had—gifts of 'the theatre', which, pejoratively, might be regarded as merely 'theatrical'. His characters easily conceive themselves in terms of stagey effect. Aspatia's instructions to her women embroidering scenes of forsaken love is characteristic:

Do it by me,
Do it by me, the lost Aspatia;
And you shall find all true but the wild island.
Suppose I stand upon the sea-beach now,
Mine arms thus, and mine hair blown with the wind,
Wild as that desert; and let all about me
Tell that I am forsaken. Do my face
(If thou had'st ever feeling for a sorrow)
Thus, thus, Antiphila: strive to make me look
Like Sorrow's monument; and the trees about me,
Let them be dry and leafless; let the rocks
Groan with continual surges; and behind me,
Make all a desolation. See, see, wenches,
A miserable life of this poor picture.

(II, ii)

Aspatia's speech is one of the most successful poetic occasions in the play. The situations, when they break, leave behind them various and quite discrete bases on which the separate stances, monumental or heroic, can be taken. Beamont likes to arrange the situations that provide the opportunities for the stances.

The Maid's Tragedy is a more shapely play than *Philaster*. It is named after Aspatia, the forsaken maiden who seems a subordinate figure, not after Evadne, the fatal woman who dominates the action. Because of its subordinate nature, the tragedy of Aspatia is apt to be overlooked. Aspatia's tragedy does, however, frame the whole play. It springs like an arch from the introduction in Acts I and II to the dénouement of Act V. As we shall see, there were important (maybe half-conscious) reasons why Beaumont stressed the Aspatia role rather than that of his own White Devil. Yet in spite of these, it is that part of the play which centres round Evadne—Evadne, Amintor, and the King—which looms largest. It is in this part that Beaumont's 'servile *jure divino* royalism' finds its expression. It is here also that his King is killed. The significance of either can only be seen in regard to the relationship in which each stands to each, and in regard to something more inclusive than either—something typical of Beaumont (particularly) as a dramatist, and symptomatic (through him) of a time.

Aspatia has been affianced to Amintor, and Amintor has fully intended to marry her. When the play opens, however, Aspatia is already the forsaken. The King has commanded Amintor to marry Evadne instead. Evadne, unknown to Amintor, is the King's mistress. Amintor knows her only as a very beautiful woman, and the sister of his friend Melantius. The broken promise weighs lightly at this point on Amintor's conscience. Aspatia had, he says, 'my promise',

> *but the King forbad it*
> *And made me make this worthy change.* (I, i)

The King's order, Evadne's own attractiveness, and the fact that she is Melantius's sister—Melantius is the soul of honour and a victorious general just returning from the wars—are all factors that might excuse his fickleness. Amintor, anyway, experiences no compunction until the moment when he is about to join Evadne on the first night of their marriage:

> *I did that lady wrong. Methinks I feel*
> *A grief shoot suddenly through all my veins;*
> *Mine eyes rain: this is strange at such a time.*
> *It was the King first moved me to't; but he*

Has not my will in keeping. Why do I
Perplex myself thus? Something whispers me
Go not to bed. My guilt is not so great
As mine own conscience too sensible
Would make me think; I only brake a promise,
And 'twas the King enforced me. Timorous flesh,
Why shak'st thou so? Away, my idle fears.

(II, i)

The *sudden* grief, here, shooting through *all* his veins, the inability to see it except as something *strange*; the comparative thinness of the rationalization, and the taking refuge in the King's injunction; the deliberate action of the will in its effort after suppression—all this is typical of the Beaumont hero. The past seems to have a delayed action, but the action, like a time-bomb's, is inevitable. And when the past does explode into the present, as it does here, it first divides the mind and then brings about a new kind of consciousness, a new and guiltier deliberacy. But a great perversion is taking place. The moral choice is merely now consciously to ratify a guilty act done formerly without sufficient deliberation. The will is exerted, so to speak, merely to turn past mistakes into present sins: to write-off the losses once they are realized, and to give itself over more completely to error.

Amintor, then, in this acute state of self-division, pauses on the threshold. Evadne—already prepared for bed—comes out to join him. Immediately on seeing her Amintor is swept away into rapturous anticipations of the hymeneal. That he should give himself so completely and so quickly to this opposite mood is not out-of-character. Nor is it out of harmony with Beaumont's controlling conception. The joy shoots as suddenly through Amintor as did the grief. And both come from the same ambivalent source.

Beaumont intends in this scene a witty conceit. Starting from here he will conduct us to the final departure of Evadne and Amintor into their bedroom. The foul conditions attached to the marriage fully revealed, Amintor the lover will go off as Amintor the cuckold: resolved to show the world every appearance of fulfilment while he hides from it, at the same time, his inner frustration. The audience will see the pair enter their bedroom like a bride and groom. They will know, however, that everything else is the reverse of what they expected:

AMINTOR. *as wantonly*
As ever longing bride and bridegroom met,
Let's laugh and enter here.
EVADNE. *I am content.*
AMINTOR. *Down all the swellings of my troubled heart!*
When we walk thus entwined, let all eyes see
If ever lovers better did agree.

In the conduct of this elaborate turn Beaumont is able to bring off what are sometimes taken for perversions of character to situation, or of emotional coherence to rhetorical opportunity, but which, I think, are better regarded as so many moral puns. He achieves something more important than mere surprises, more significant than stage-tricks; something which has to do with his feeling for radical dislocation—a dislocation which can express itself in incongruities macabre, comic, or harrowing as the occasion demands. We might look at some of these main turns in more detail.

The first is when Evadne refuses to go in. Amintor thinks that this is 'but the coyness of a bride'. There is coolness and contempt, and a struggle between boredom and impatience in Evadne's reply:

EVADNE. *The coyness of a bride!*
AMINTOR. *How prettily*
That frown becomes thee!

There is nothing more tiresome than such gauche and misplaced flirtatiousness. Evadne is soon provoked to irritate Amintor out of his playfulness into a vague uneasiness, before finally precipitating him deftly into indignation and heroics—against the man Amintor thinks has somehow wronged her. It is then that Evadne drops her bombshell:

Now I shall try thy truth. If thou dost love me,
Thou weigh'st not anything compared with me:
Life, honour, joys eternal, all delights
This world can yield, or hopeful people feign,
Or in the life to come, are light as air
To a true lover when his lady frowns,
And bids him do this. *Wilt thou kill this man?*
Swear, my Amintor, and I'll kiss the sin
Off from thy lips.

AMINTOR. *I will not swear, sweet love,*
Till I do know the cause.

EVADNE. *I would thou could'st.*
Why, it is thou that wrong'st me; I hate thee;
Thou should'st have killed thyself.

Appearance-and-reality is percurrent as a theme in Beaumont. In this passage appearance takes on punning resemblances to reality, and pun is interlocked with pun. What Amintor imagines to be a coy bride is in reality the King's mistress. What Amintor imagines is some other man, and what even the audience is led to guess might be the King, both audience and Amintor discover in the end to be Amintor himself: it is suicide rather than honourable murder that is called for. As far as this, we are on the familiar ground of Beaumont's ironies. Similar manipulations of the expected and unexpected run through the scene in *Philaster* between Philaster and Bellario. Further puns, however, are mounted within this framework. Evadne takes on herself the punning appearance of the wronged maiden Amintor thinks she must be. In doing so she mimics the accent and manner of the absolute of petrarchan love—an absolute which Amintor himself has first suggested by his heroics. Evadne forces the code to its extremest limit—'Wilt thou kill this man?' The tone of her words is mocking, incredulous, and contemptuous. She disbelieves both the petrarchan protestations of Amintor, and the Christian code with which—if he were really moved to murder—the petrarchanism would clash. Evadne's cynicism is twofold. She is aware of the blasphemies involved, and unimpressed by Amintor's wordy protestations of petrarchan faith. But further—another turn of the screw—we see the blasphemous use to which she would put Amintor's belief in his own code. She is committed to evil. She has resolved that evil will be her good. Her phrase, 'I'll kiss the sin off from thy lips' is a powerful focus for all this, and more. When the full revelation is made, and the audience knows with Amintor that it is Amintor's suicide she is demanding, and Amintor's dead lips she would kiss—with a warmth of gratitude that she could never feel for anything otherwise that he could do, and with a passion that not even lust could awaken in her—the meanings and ironies of the phrase shake into a new pattern like pieces of tinsel in a kaleidoscope. Evadne at this point achieves a Luciferian dimension of evil:

> *Wilt thou kill this man?*
> *Swear, my Amintor, and I'll kiss the sin*
> *Off from thy lips.*

The complexities and obscenities reach Black Mass proportions. In Evadne's 'my Amintor' contempt and pitying condescension mix with the tainted mockery of endearment. Beside the quickening warmth is the cold knowledge of her utter and intimidating self-possession. Amintor is a helpless tool. The quickening and the warmth are indeed real. Evadne has an almost necrophilic affection for the prospect of Amintor sacrificing himself in this cause. In 'kiss the sin off from thy lips' she arrogates to herself the power of absolution for what she knows is an unpardonable offence. The blasphemous and the necrophilic combine. The perversion of love and gratitude involved deliberately breaks bonds human and divine. Evadne is so convincingly presented now as to make credible the final routing of Amintor, emotionally, intellectually, and morally. Amintor's last throw is to threaten her with physical violence—his final assertion of independence and manhood. Evadne counters by telling him her lover is the King:

EVADNE. *What wilt you do now?*
AMINTOR. *'Tis not the King!*
EVADNE. *What did he make the match for, dull Amintor?*
AMINTOR. *Oh thou hast named a word that wipes away*

All thoughts revengeful! In that sacred word,
'The King,' there lies a terror: what frail man
Dares lift his hand against it? Let the gods
Speak to him when they please: till then, let us
Suffer and wait.

In the rest of the scene Amintor seems to shrivel visibly. He becomes the empty husk of the heroic. At the absolute limit of his debasement he sounds again the note of bewilderment, of amazement at himself, of puzzlement over his own incomprehensibility: a repetition at a deeper level of his reactions at the very beginning of the scene when the memory of Aspatia came into his mind. Beaumont seizes the opportunity to make a further pun, or series of puns:

AMINTOR. *What strange thing am I!*
EVADNE. *A miserable one; one that myself*
Am sorry for.
AMINTOR. *Why, show it then in this:*
If thou hast pity, though thy love be none,
Kill me; and all true lovers, that shall live
In after ages crossed in their desires,
Shall bless thy memory, and call thee good,
Because such mercy in thy love was found,
To rid a lingering wretch.
EVADNE. *I must have one*
To fill thy room again, if thou wert dead;
Else, by this night, I would! I pity thee.

Amintor who has refused Evadne's request that he should commit suicide is now making the request that Evadne should slay him: that suicide without self-slaughter which most of Beaumont's tragic characters are bent on. There are puns within puns in this parody of the petrarchan situation. In this latter, the ardent lover prays to his chaste mistress to put him out of his pain, and save him from mortal illness by acquiescence. Here Amintor is filled with loathing, prays for death rather than relief, and addresses himself to a wanton he has married and must not possess: a complete and monstrous inversion of the petrarchan. Such an inversion, too, is the pun on the future lovers, crossed in love, who will look back on Evadne's mercy-killing and bless her for it. The greatest pun of all, however, is Evadne's 'pity':

I must have one
To fill thy room again, if thou wert dead;
Else, by this night, I would! I pity thee.

What makes for hideousness here is that Evadne's pity is, again, real—a warmth of compassion that turns the normal upside-down. For normally we feel pity when we must do some hurt in a good cause; and then the hurt (the evil) is embraced by the compassion, and the element of evil is redeemed by this embrace. In Evadne's mood the sincere and compulsive pity is embraced by an icy evil:

I must have one
To fill thy room again, if thou wert dead.

Such pity is a refinement of the diabolical and macabre. Even compassion is reconciled with the wilful inversion of human kindness Evadne is resolved upon. It is a witty and even credible juxtaposition of incompatibles, of holy and unholy. All that is necessary for the scene now is its ending, Evadne and Amintor going off into their bedroom mutually 'entwined':

Come, let us practise, and, as wantonly
As ever longing bride and bridegroom met
Let's laugh and enter here.

As a study in radical perversity Evadne is more compelling than Lady Macbeth, and more subtle. If she is not a profounder study that is because Lady Macbeth stands in a perspective of profundities. She is one term in a complex that includes Macbeth, the Witches, and the Shakespearian metaphysic of Nature, Time and Eternity. Beaumont's universe, for all its external complication and wit, is, in the end, a simplification. The moral pun implies simplification. The disparate absolutes brought together are fragmentations of a less consciously formulable, more inclusive traditional scheme. The apparent complication also means a real coarsening. A code or schema that can be so readily attitudinized is likely also to be all the more limited because of the over-emphasis it assumes. The simple thing behind the splintering world is the need just for such divisions as the plays present. There is something profoundly significant, however, in the displacement of concreteness involved, in the way persons are required constantly to subordinate themselves to arbitrary external systems or portions of systems, the whole submitting to the part. Amintor's complete dissociation in the scene we have so far looked at is expressive of a general dissociation in the dramatist, too. Amintor cries, when his shattering is complete:

> *These strange and sudden injuries have fallen*
> *So thick upon me, that I lose all sense*
> *Of what they are. Methinks, I am not wronged;*
> *Nor is it aught if from the censuring world*
> *I can but hide it. Reputation*
> *Thou art a word, no more.*

The effect here is not a cheap one, and the capacity to present such bewilderment, so accurately, an unenviable gift of birth rather than education. It is Othello being made to speak with the voice of Iago, the lion reduced to wearing the fox's skin. Beaumont risks many a fall in his attempts continually to walk such tight-ropes as these. Here his daring and his skill enbale him not only to walk but to pirouette on the wire. Shakespeare's interest in the ambiguities of appearance and reality, his concern with the paradox of hypocrisy, finds a resting-place ultimately in the assertion of *some* certainties that patiently endure. The appearances only derive their power from the realities they mock. But, for Shakespeare,

> *Angels are bright still, though the brightest fell,*
> *Though all things foul should wear the brows of grace,*
> *Yet grace must still look so.* (*Macbeth*, IV. iii. 22–4)

Beaumont makes no such assertions. He has cut the tap-root that always steadied the popular drama in the traditional assurances. Appearance now mirrors appearance in an endless hall of mirrors. In place of the traditional patience there is merely the real and 'modern' homelessness, the paralysing vision of appearances endlessly self-repeating, and the manipulation of the mirror-images, by wit, for present effect.

There is a further side of Evadne yet to be revealed. It amounts to another exciting conceit in terms of situation. Beaumont has used the King and Evadne to shatter Amintor. Now he will use Evadne and Amintor to divide the King. Evadne and Amintor act their happy marriage too convincingly. When he visits them next morning the King is alarmed at what he sees. He takes Evadne aside to interrogate her:

KING. *How do you like Amintor?*
EVADNE. *As I did, sir.*
KING. *How's that?*
EVADNE. *As one that, to fulfil your pleasure,*
I have given leave to call me wife and love.
KING. *I see there is no lasting faith in sin;*
They that break word with heaven will break again
With all the world, and so thou dost with me.
EVADNE. *How, sir?*
KING. *This subtle woman's ignorance*
Will not excuse you: thou hast taken oaths,
So great, methought, they did not well become
A woman's mouth, that thou wouldst ne'er enjoy
A man but me.
EVADNE. *I never did swear so;*
You do me wrong.
KING. *Day and night have heard it.*
EVADNE. *I swore indeed that I would never love*
A man of lower place; but, if your fortune
Should throw you from this height, I bade you trust
I would forsake you, and would bend to him,
That won your throne: I love with my ambition,
Not with my eyes. But, if I ever yet
Touched any other, leprosy light here
Upon my face! which for your royalty
I would not stain. (III. i.)

The King cannot believe her, however, even when she pleads the grounds of self-interest for her faithfulness. He threatens her with his extremest displeasure, and Evadne is forced to call in Amintor. It is a witty inversion of role for all three concerned: the King jealous and believing himself cuckolded; Evadne indignant and virtuous; Amintor able to dictate the game.

EVADNE. *Amintor, thou hast an ingenious look,*
And shouldst be virtuous: it amazeth me
That thou canst make such base malicious lies!
AMINTOR. *What, my dear wife?*
EVADNE. *Dear wife! I do despise thee.*
Why, nothing can be baser than to sow
Dissention amongst lovers.
AMINTOR. *Lovers! who?*
EVADNE. *The King and me!*

This final humiliation Amintor sees as a further turn of the screw. The faithless sin he made to fair Aspatia is not yet revenged: it follows him. His outburst, however, convinces the King of Evadne's reliability, though it is so violent the King has now to threaten Amintor with punishment. To this Amintor replies:

If you have any worth, for Heavens sake, think
I fear not swords; for, as you are mere man,
I dare as easily kill you for this deed,
As you dare think to do it. But there is
Divinity about you, that strikes dead
My rising passions: as you are my King,
I fall before you, and present my sword
To cut my own flesh.

Amintor is boxed in, in the last resort, by his 'servile *jure divino* royalism'. Evadne, as we have seen, is neither servile, nor passively obedient. She is royalist only in that she loves with her ambition and nothing below a throne will content her. The King himself is portrayed throughout as merely a person. He has absolute power, but the absolutism is diminished to the political only. Nothing naturally regal or supernaturally sanctioned invests him in fact. Although Amintor asserts that there is divinity about him, he is the worst of tyrants. One other main figure in the play must now be brought in before Beaumont's '*jure divino* royalism' can be seen clearly for what it is: viz. one among several competing codes, rather than a moral scheme basic to the play as a whole. This figure is Melantius—the Beaumontian soldier type, victorious, Evadne's brother, and Amintor's greatest friend.

Melantius stands for Honour—the honour among men who have been comrades in arms, family honour, and the honour due to the Soldier as such. It is the Soldier who maintains the State. Even the King depends on him:

And for you, my King,
Your subjects all have fed by virtue of
My arm: this sword of mine hath ploughed the ground,
And reaped the fruit in peace;
And you yourself have lived at home in ease.

(IV. ii.)

The Soldier demobbed must suffer the indignities and insults of the peace:

It is the curse of soldiers, that in peace
They shall be braved by such ignoble men
As, if the land were troubled, would with tears
And knees beg succour from 'em.

(I. i.)

In the court he returns to he meets

a race of idle people . . .
Facers and talkers, to defame the worth
Of those that do things worthy. (I. i.)

The Soldier is outside the State. He is its creator and maintainer. He preserves, for Beaumont, one fixed point from which comment, criticism, and decisive action can come. Beaumont is even aware (though this insight is not in *The Maid's Tragedy*) that the Soldier's Honour is a kind of narrow madness, a reflection of the destructive and conflicting insanities of the mad world he comes back to from his campaigns. The Soldier in *A King and No King* cries out in exasperation:

Give me the wars, where men
Are mad, and may talk what they list, and held
The bravest fellows; this pelting, prattling peace
Is good for nothing; drinking's a virtue to 't.

Melantius in *The Maid's Tragedy*, however, is not merely exasperated. He is moved to revulsion and revolt.

Melantius senses that something is wrong with Amintor. He gets Amintor to divulge the story of the 'marriage'. It is a scene (III, ii) intended to be as witty in its moral puns—its clash of opposed loyalties: friendship, family honour, personal faith, belief in the King—as that between Evadne and Amintor. But Beaumont here is less adroit. The scene does, however, end with a witty paradox. When Melantius is persuaded of his sister's whoredom he swears at once to kill the King:

The credit of our house is thrown away.
But from his den I'll waken Death,
And hurl him on this King: my honesty
Shall steel my sword; and on its horrid point
I'll wear my cause, that shall amaze the eyes
Of this proud man, and be too glittering
For him to look on.

Amintor's reaction is, of course, to forbid it. He draws his sword. The two friends now face each other as enemies, and the quarrel would be impossible if they were not profoundly pledged to friendship. However, the duel does not take place. Melantius promises he will not kill the King. But in his mind there is a mental reservation Amintor cannot guess at. Melantius intends to see Evadne, to convince her of her wickedness, and make her the executioner.

This scene between Amintor and Melantius is the turning point of the play. From now on the interest is maintained more by the external movement of the plot than by the internal pressure of the wit and the moral punning of the separate scenes. Evadne, for example, confronted by either Amintor or the King, has been hitherto an intimidating and impregnable figure of evil, cold, powerful, and self-assured. She is broken down in the interview with her brother by Melantius's physical violence rather than by his moral persuasiveness. The morality, in fact, of what Melantius would demand, she sees, in any case, as—at the least—doubtful:

EVADNE. *I feel*
Too many sad confusions here, to let in
Any loose glance hereafter.
MELANTIUS. *Dost thou not feel, 'mongst all those, one brave anger*
That breaks out nobly, and directs thine arm
To kill this base King?
EVADNE. *All the gods forbid it!*
MELANTIUS. *No, all the gods require it!*
They are dishonoured in him. . . .
You're valiant in his bed, and bold enough
To be a stale whore . . . thus far you know
No fear. Come, you shall kill him. (IV. i.)

And Melantius forces his sister to swear she will murder the King, to wipe out her own and her family's dishonour. Sin thus will cancel sin.

The dramatic interest in the second half of the play is well maintained. There is the clever trick whereby Melantius forces Clianax, the Keeper of the fort, and his sworn enemy, to yield up the fortress. It is a comic handling of the theme of appearance and reality. Melantius plays the classical game of the Machiavel. He adds a further refinement to it, nevertheless. Edgar, so to speak, is present (and equally helpless) while Edmund is blackening him to Gloster. There is also the scene between the repentant Evadne and Amintor. This ends in a finely portrayed reconcilement and forgiveness. At this point it looks as if a new moral basis is to be given to the action of the play. Evadne recognizes, and Amintor invokes, the traditional sanctions:

EVADNE. *I am hell*
Till you, my dear lord, shoot your light into me,
The beams of your forgiveness; I am soul-sick,
And wither with the fear of one condemned,
Till I have got your pardon.

AMINTOR. *Rise Evadne.*
Those heavenly powers that put this good into thee
Grant a continuance of it! I forgive thee:
Make thyself worthy of it; and take heed,
Take heed, Evadne, this be serious.
Mock not the powers above, that can and dare
Give thee a great example of their justice
To all ensuing ages, if thou playest
With thy repentance, the best sacrifice.

EVADNE. *I have done nothing good to win belief,*
My life hath been so faithless. . . .
I will redeem one minute of my age
Or like another Niobe, I'll weep,
Till I am water.

AMINTOR. *I am now dissolved. . . .*
My frozen soul melts. May each sin thou hast
Find a new mercy! Rise, I am at peace. . . .
My charity shall go along with thee,
Though my embraces must be far from thee. (IV. i.)

However, the play is not calculated to move to any such happy conclusion as this reconciliation indicates. Evadne must commit the crime of killing the King. Amintor must meet with his past, too, in the person of Aspatia disguised as a boy: Aspatia pretending to be her own brother come from the wars to avenge her. Aspatia must be mortally wounded by Amintor in a duel, there must be the discovery by Amintor of what he has done, Amintor's suicide, and in the end the succession to the throne of a just King rather than a tyrant, with the pardoning of Melantius. The new King's final words are equable and stern:

bear those bodies in.
May this a fair example be to me,
To rule with temper; for on lustful Kings
Unlooked-for sudden deaths from heaven are sent;
But cursed is he that is their instrument. (V. iv.)

It has the sound of something commonplace, unconceited, sensible, and traditional.

* * *

We have dismissed the latter half of the play rather summarily, and concentrated on the central core of the tragedy which concerns Amintor, Evadne, the King and Melantius, in their main relations to each other. It is in these relations that Beaumont is most engaged. In these the interests and skills peculiar to him among the Elizabethans are best displayed. A second reason for passing over the last two acts is that, as we have indicated, the issues there returned to are familiar and traditional. Like *Philaster*, *The Maid's Tragedy* surrounds its central petrarchanism with the great commonplaces which run through the popular drama of Shakespeare and the Globe. In *The Maid's Tragedy* as in *Philaster* these themes, however, are marginal concerns.

In examining the central situations we have stressed the underlying Wit in their conception. The play is contrived to put on the stage a succession of brilliant and gruesome moral puns. It is not a question of a simple sensationalism. Beaumont is wrongly understood if his greatest scenes are dismissed with the formula that everything here—character, moral coherence, poetic integrity—is sacrificed to 'situation'. Such a judgment has come, I think, from two things: first, the inapplicability to his work of the Bradleyan assumptions (much more so, in his case, than in Shakespeare's); second, the equal inapplicability of what in our time has replaced the Bradleyan approach, viz. verbal analysis, the examination of recurrent images, the exposition of dramatic unity as a poetic unity revealed best in the symphonic treatment of a number of assorted themes. Beaumont's stage-personalities are of course people, but they are not characters. The kind of Coleridgean 'Key-note' that would reveal them as harmonic unities is missing. They are the sort of people who are not, and cannot be, unified. Beaumont, in fact, is only interested in disunity. His people are fragmented by the choices they have to make. And the fragments must still live on, to occupy the stage and conduct their story to its end: as sometimes also happens in real life. Similarly, Beaumont's verse passes through the filters of verbal analysis. It displays no variegated sensibility. It has no local knottings of thought and feeling. The knots are tied, in Beaumont's case, by *situation*. The verse can afford to be simple and straightforward. The wit works with moral rather than verbal puns. More than even Shakespeare does, Beaumont needs the stage to display his greatness: a whole succession of scenes rather than any single speech. And the wit is baroque. The contortionate violences are accompanied by a cool, deliberate, intellectual manipulation. The audience can be detached and roused to passionate sympathies both at the same time.

The charge that Beaumont sacrifices everything to situation, combined with the acknowledgment of his skill in contriving situation, might suggest that he is not quite sincere. There can, however, be little doubt as to the seriousness with which Beaumont took himself and his themes. There is in fact something obsessional in his main concern. The sameness of his types in the three most characteristic plays (*A King and No King* goes with *Philaster* and *The Maid's Tragedy*) indicates obsession rather than poverty of invention. They *are* unities, but the unity they have is schizophrenic. Beaumont insists on dividing the minds of each of his *dramatis personae*. He compels them to walk among the mirrors. Everyone is set amid conflicts no single one can contain. Choice for them means scission, and finally self-destruction. No one mind in the plays can embrace the full range of the competing and imperative absolutes that environ it. Loosed from any reason grounded in assured and public certainties, the intellect is paralysed, and the will left to work by suppressing some of the half-truths while violently asserting its adherence to others. The deepest note in Beaumont is one of negation:

> *All the happiness*
> *Bestowed upon me turns into disgrace.*
> *Gods, take your honesty again, for I*
> *Am loaden with it.* (III. ii).

We have underlined, both in Beaumont and in Fletcher, the literary inspiration of their work. They differ from Shakespeare in that they had read Shakespeare—the Shakespeare of the tragic period rather than the Shakespeare who wrote the Last Plays. *Hamlet* seems to have made the profoundest impression on Beaumont. It is echoed in *Philaster*; it reappears, too, in *The Maid's Tragedy*. The morning after his wedding night, for example, Amintor meets his loyal friend Melantius. He says:

I wonder much, Melantius,
To see those noble looks, that make me think
How virtuous thou art: and, in the sudden,
'Tis strange to me thou shouldst have worth and honour;
Or not be base, and false, and treacherous,
And every ill. . . . Oh, mistake me not!
I know thee to be full of all those deeds
That we frail men call good; but, by the course
Of nature thou shouldst be as quickly changed
As are the winds; dissembling as the sea,
That now wears brows as smooth as virgins' be,
Tempting the merchant to invade his face,
And in an hour calls his billows up,
And shoots 'em at the sun, destroying all
He carries on him. (III. ii.)

And, later, the impossibility of deciding between appearance and reality has gone further:

Man's eyes are not so subtle to perceive
My inward misery: I bear my grief
Hid from the world. How art thou wretchéd then?
For aught I know, all husbands are like me;
For every one I talk with of his wife
Is but a well dissembler of his woes
As I am. Would I knew it! for the rareness
Afflicts me now. (III. ii.)

Beaumont's knowledge of Shakespearian tragedy was as important for him as his reading in Sidney's *Arcadia*. And in each case it is an active use of his forerunners that we have—not an obsequious following, or a random echoing. Beaumont seizes on the one great tragedy of Shakespeare which stands nearest his own in mood and content, in moral bewilderment and confusion. Hamlet, too, like Amintor, would welcome a road out of the impasse which appearance and reality, and their indistinguishability, constitute. Hamlet, too, is afflicted by the ridiculousness of hypocrisy's being so far general, and the hypocrites so successful, that everyone is the same, and yet everyone labours under his singularity, is afflicted with his own 'rareness'. Beaumont, so to speak, fixes on that aspect of *Hamlet* which illuminates his own central concern. And his use of Shakespeare (it amounts to a further progression into the *Hamlet* blind alley) throws light on something in Shakespeare, too.

The literary sophistication, the technique of the moral pun, the element of large-scale metaphysical conceit in Beaumont, seem to argue a different kind of audience for his plays. This audience cannot be a highly mixed one. Nor is it based on the broad and commonplace sanities of the popular tradition. It is an audience, rather, in comparison with the Globe audience, sectional, homogeneous, and sophisticated: such an audience, in fact, as has been imagined for Blackfriars after 1608—the wealthier section of what had once attended the Globe; an audience predominantly drawn from the Court, and the fringes of Whitehall; a mixture of younger sons, demobbed captains, place-seekers, sycophants, scholars, readers of Donne, 'facers and talkers'. The Victorians liked to paint the pictures of James's Court and Beaumont's admirers as black as possible. There is no need, however, to follow their exaggerations in detail. It is sufficient to agree that the new audience is narrower, more partisan than the old, less mixed and less in touch with the Elizabethan tradition—that tradition which gave the Globe audience its vital unity. Beaumont not only used his literary sources. He used, too, those features in his social environment which provided him with the absolutes that precipitated the conflicts and divisions his view of things required. The elements of division were around him. The historical situation, as we have said, was one in which fissure was becoming more and more apparent. The absolutes of loyalty, as an external requirement, to King or Parliament, High Church or Low, Spain or Holland, were clamant and objective. Beaumont's personal concerns imaged something in the external situation. This ensured for his presentations a maybe immediate and probably excessive popularity He could speak for his time more excitingly and tragically and irresponsibly than could Shakespeare, writing for all time.

What was happening with Beaumont can be seen most clearly, I think, in his own terms. He is curiously aware of what he is doing, even when he seems most unconscious of his own drift. We shall need to turn back to his play again for the final statement.

There are two fixed points in *The Maid's Tragedy*. One is Melantius, the returned Soldier; the other is Aspatia, the forsaken maiden. The two form an arch within an arch spanning the central group of Amintor, Evadne, the King. Melantius himself occupies firmly the immovable platform of Honour—a soldier Honour which survives the clash of the absolutes (Honour itself is one such absolute), but this same Honour breaks Evadne and nullifies her Christian repentance as well as Amintor's Christian forgiveness of her, and it ends by destroying Evadne, the King himself, and (indirectly) Amintor, too. Like Melantius, Aspatia stands on immovable ground. She occupies a position, however, remote from the immediate emotional and moral interests of the dramatist, however necessary she is for the mechanics of the play—necessary for the play to have a beginning and to have an end.

Aspatia figures mainly in the very beginning of the play and in the very end. Yet she is of more than marginal importance for understanding Beaumont. It must have been almost by instinct that he called the play after her rather than after Evadne, casting his final glance on the jilted girl rather than on the fatal woman. Aspatia represents that large and immovable continent of the traditional morality from which the 'wild island' of Beaumont's dramatic world detaches itself, and floats away to the destruction of all concerned save one. Amintor has been faithless to Aspatia. Evadne has wandered and desperately lost herself. The King has forsaken true Kingship for foul tyranny. All three (and Aspatia, too) are destroyed. Only Melantius, the soldier whose Honour is greater even than his loyalty to the throne, survives the general disaster.

But Melantius's 'Honour', like Amintor's 'servile *jure divino* royalism' is merely one of the false absolutes which bemuse and destroy their adherents. It is nearer to the traditional decencies, certainly, but its real element is the simplifying madness of war —war as the expression and only possible container of the insensate follies and perversities the returning soldier finds in the corrupt civilian world he safeguards, feeds, and despises. It is Aspatia, the world of simple traditional values, who is destroyed in the play, not Melantius. Melantius survives to preside over the fortunes and welfare of the future King.

Beaumont was right, therefore, to call his play after Aspatia. *The Maid's Tragedy* is what happens when Aspatia, out of deference for a *jure divino* absolutist's command, is almost casually forsaken. At the beginning of the play she paints her own picture. Like Arethusa's in *Philaster*, it is both powerfully moving and capable of immediate application to the play generally. She sees herself standing like Dido after Aeneas deserted her. The scene around her is blasted and desolate, a wilderness in which all get lost, an unreality that becomes an agonizing nightmare. She knows she is deserted. She knows, too, that those who have deserted her have deserted themselves. The deep undertone of Beaumont's play is audible if, at the end, we turn back to Aspatia's pathetic speech at the beginning—those lines which Mr. T. S. Eliot (one of his profoundest and most critical perceptions of Beaumont's place in his own time and his relevance for ours) put as a motto to one of his early poems:

You shall find all true but the wild island,
Suppose I stand upon the sea-beach now,
Mine arms thus, and mine hair blown by the wind,
Wild as that desert; and let all about me
Tell that I am forsaken. Do my face
(If thou hadst ever feeling for a sorrow)
Thus, thus, Antiphila: strive to make me look
Like sorrow's monument; and the trees about me,
Let them be dry and leafless; let the rocks
Groan with continual surges; and behind me,
Make all a desolation. See, see, wenches,
A miserable life of this poor picture.

(II. ii.)

Notes

PROLOGUE

1. See J. W. Saunders, 'The Stigma of Print, A Note on the Social Bases of Tudor Poetry': *Essays in Criticism*, Vol. I, p. 139.

CHAPTER ONE

1. Edmund Gosse, *Life and Letters of John Donne*, Vol. 1, p. 191.
2. Ibid.
3. John Aubrey, *Brief Lives* (Ed. A. Clark), Vol. 1, p. 314.
4. Fulke Greville, *Life of Sir Philip Sidney* (Ed. Nowell Smith), p. 176.
5. E. Greenlaw, *Studies in Spenser's Historical Allegory*, p. 112 *seq.*
6. Shakespeare, *Sonnet* 64.
7. Op. cit., p. 10.
8. S. Daniel, 'Philotas', II, 1676–85: *Works* (Ed. A. B. Grosart), Vol. III.
9. Op. cit., p. 192.
10. Op. cit., p. 202.
11. Op. cit., p. 179.
12. *Timon of Athens*, III, iii, 145–74. (Line references as in *Complete Works*, Ed. W. J. Craig, Oxford Edn.)
13. Op. cit., p. 15.
14. J. Bronowski, *Poet's Defence*.
15. Op. cit., p. 18.
16. Op. cit., pp. 153–4.
17. *Brief Lives*, II, p. 248.
18. 'The Shepherd's Calendar', April.
19. John Donne, 'To the Countess of Huntingdon', *Complete Poetry*, etc. (Nonesuch Edn.), p. 171
20. Op. cit., p. 231.
21. Gosse, Vol. II, p. 79.
22. *The Works of Ben Jonson* (Ed. Wm. Gifford), Vol. III, p. 471.
23. Phoebe Sheavyn, *The Literary Profession in the Elizabethan Age*, p. 22.
24. Gosse, Vol. I, p. 165.
25. Gosse, Vol. I, p. 181.
26. Donne, pp., 170–1.
27. *Private Memoirs of Sir Kenelm Digby* (Ed. Sir Harris Nicolas), p. 56.

28. Op. cit., p. 65.
29. *Works*, Vol. III, p. 298.
30. Op. cit., Vol. III, p. 484.
31. Op. cit., Vol. III, p. 499.
32. Op. cit., Vol. III, p. 264.

CHAPTER TWO

1. G. M. Trevelyan, *England Under the Stuarts*, Note, pp. 45–6.
2. J. Milton, *Works* (Bohn Edn.), Vol. I, pp. 327–8.
3. Greville, p. 16.
4. Sir Philip Sidney, *An Apologie for Poetry:* in *Preface to Poetry* (Everyman), p. 27.
5. Sir Philip Sidney, *The Countess of Pembroke's Arcadia* (Ed. Ernest A. Baker), p. 322.
6. Op. cit., p. 5.
7. Op. cit., p. 20.
8. Op. cit., p. 46.
9. Op. cit., p. 352.
10. Sir William Temple, *Miscellanea* (5th Edn., 1697), Vol. II, p. 335.
11. Op. cit., p. 10.
12. Op. cit., p. 15.
13. Op. cit., p. 43.
14. Op. cit., p. 42.
15. Op. cit., p. 60.
16. Op. cit., p. 61.
17. Op. cit., p. 13.
18. Op. cit., p. 140.
19. Op. cit., pp. 312–3.
20. Op. cit., p. 317.
21. Op. cit., p. 318.
22. Op. cit., p. 320.
23. See Ronald B. Levinson, 'The "Godlesse Minde" in Sidney's "Arcadia" ', *Mod. Phil.*, xxix, p. 21.
24. See Kenneth Muir and John F. Danby, ' "Arcadia" and "King Lear" ', *Notes and Queries*, Vol. 195, p. 49.
25. Op. cit., p. 341.
26. Op. Cit., p. 402.
27. See Kenneth Thorpe Rowe, 'Romantic Love and Parental Authority in Sidney's "Arcadia" ', *Univ. of Michigan Contributions in Modern Philology No.* 4.
28. Op. cit., p. 547.
29. Op. cit., pp. 592–3.
30. Op. cit., p. 595.
31. Op. cit., p. 557.

CHAPTER THREE

1. T. S. Eliot, *The Use of Poetry and the Use of Criticism*, p. 51.
2. Mona Wilson, *Sir Philip Sidney*, p. 140.

3. *Arcadia*, p. 587.
4. Op. cit., p. 564.
5. Op. cit., pp. 203–6.
6. Op. cit., pp. 269–70.
7. Op. cit., p. 225.
8. Op. cit., p. 117.
9. *Paradise Lost*, Bk. ix, II, 28–53.
10. Op. cit., p. 383. Zelmane is the name of Pyrocles in his woman's disguise.
11. Boethius, translated by Chaucer: *Works* (Ed. W. W. Skeat), p. 141.
12. Op. cit., p. 190.
13. *Paradise Lost*, Bk. ii, II, 28–33.
14. Op. cit., pp. 159–60.
15. E. M. W. Tillyard, *Shakespeare's Last Plays*, p. 23.
16. G. Wilson Knight, *The Crown of Life*, p. 54.
17. Op. cit. *passim*.
18. D. G. James, *The Life of Reason*, p. 138 *seq*.

CHAPTER FOUR

1. T. S. Eliot, *Selected Essays*, pp. 128–9.
2. *Works of Coverdale* (Ed. for The Parker Society): *Fruitful Lessons*, etc., pp. 175–7.
3. Roger Hutchinson, 'The Second Sermon of Oppression, Affliction, and Patience' in *Works* (Ed. for The Parker Society), p. 320.
4. Chaucer, *Works*, p. 699.
5. Op. cit., p. 320.
6. *Fruitful Lessons*, etc., pp. 261–2.
7. Op. cit., p. 305.
8. Chaucer, *Works*, p. 521.
9. Op. cit., p. 681.
10. Op. cit., p. 691.
11. Op. cit., p. 698.
12. Op. cit., p. 611.
13. Op. cit., p. 611.
14. Op. cit., p. 611.
15. Op. cit., p. 608.
16. Thomas Becon, *Works* (Ed. for The Parker Society): *Catechism*, etc., pp. 186–90.
20. Op. cit., p. 443.
21. Op. cit., p. 138.
22. Op. cit., p. 97.
23. Op. cit., p. 137.
24. Op. cit., p. 147.
25. Op. cit., p. 190.
26. Op. cit., p. 169.
27. Op. cit., p. 185.
28. Op. cit., p. 323.
29. Op. cit., p. 153.
30. Op. cit., p. 164.

CHAPTER SIX

1. S. T. Coleridge, *Lectures on Shakespeare* (Bohn Edn), p. 400.
2. Charles Lamb, *Specimens of English Dramatic Poetry:* Note on *Two Noble Kinsmen.*
3. Una Ellis-Fermor, *Jacobean Drama*, p. 207.
4. T. S. Eliot, *Selected Essays*, p. 155.
5. A. H. Thorndike, *The Influence of Beaumont and Fletcher on Shakespeare, passim.*
6. John Denham, 'On Mr Fletcher's Works'. See *The Works of Francis Beaumont and John Fletcher* (Ed. A. R. Waller), Vol. I, p. xxiii.
7. J. Berkenhead, 'On the Happy Collection of Master Fletcher's Works'. See Beaumont and Fletcher's *Works*, Vol. I, p. xli.
8. Alfred Harbage, *Cavalier Drama*, p. 22.
9. Bishop Goodman, *Court of King James* (Ed. John S. Brewer), p. 134.
10. Sir John Harington, *Nugae Antiquae* (Arr. by Rev. H. Harington, 1779), Vol. 1, p. 134.
11. Op. cit., Vol. II, p. 129.
12. John Donne, *Complete Poems*, etc. (Nonesuch Edn,), p. 122.
13. Op. cit., p. 129.
14. Op. cit., p. 6.
15. Op. cit., p. 203.
16. 'To that Noble and true Lover of Learning, Sir Walter Aston Knight', *Works*, Vol. II, p. 520.
17. Op. cit., p. 207.
18. *Nugae Antiquae*, Vol. II, p. 130.

CHAPTER SEVEN

1. Tucker Brooke, 'The Royal Fletcher and the Loyal Heywood', in *Elizabethan Studies and Other Essays in Honor of George F. Reynolds*, p. 192.
2. Op. cit., p. 194.
3. See preface to *Religio Laici.*

Index

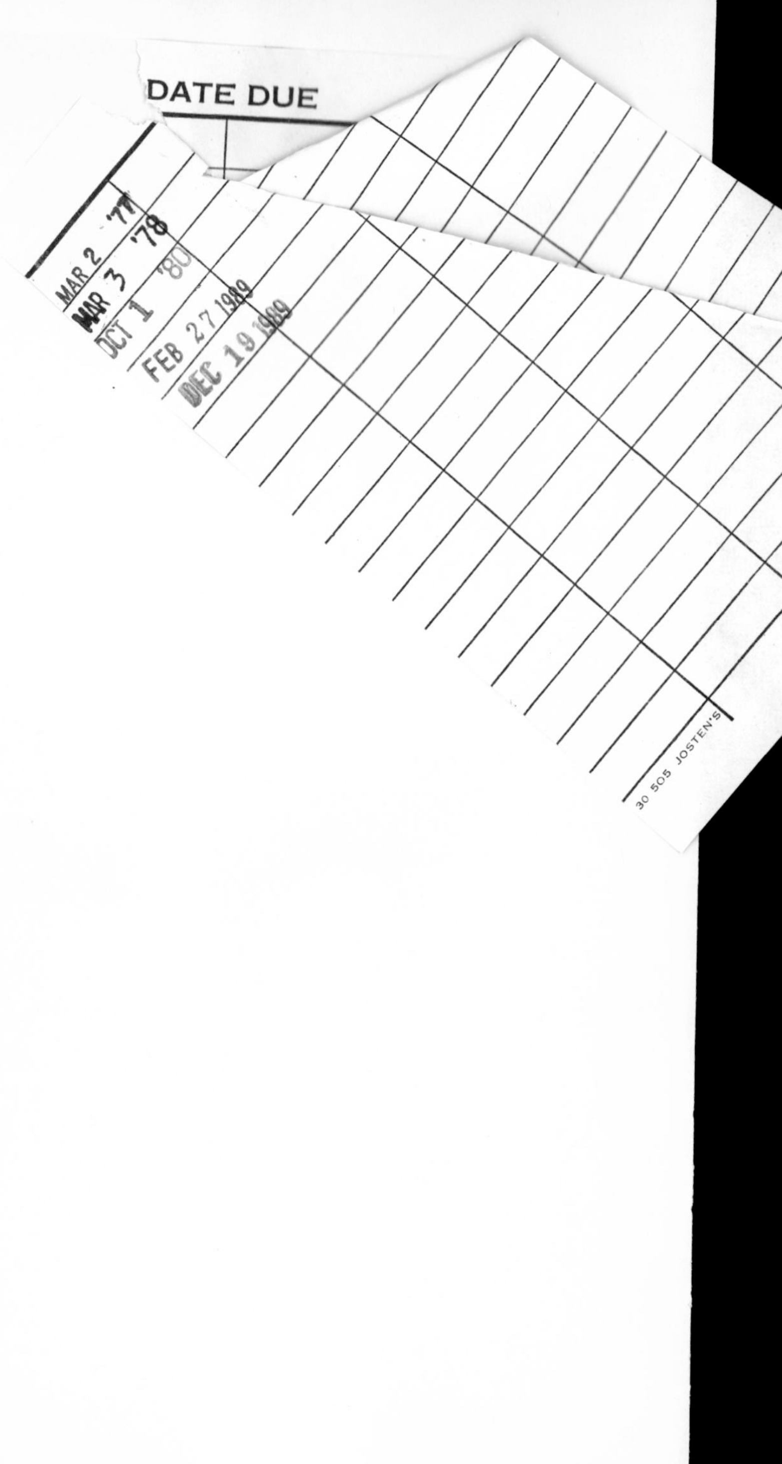
DATE DUE
MAR 2 '77
MAR 3 '78
OCT 1 '80
FEB 27 1989
DEC 19 1989
30 505 JOSTEN'S